Key Stage 1 - Number Fun

Song Resource Pack 2

by

Dave Godfrey

Omega Zone Publishing 2005

Dedication

To Timothy, Anna & Esther - our mathematically orientated children!

Like God's love, our love for you is unconditional and not based on your achievements. Your mother and I will, however, continue to celebrate all you do achieve. May the Celebration Song encourage you along the way!

Thank you to Menna, Rachel, Monica, Michael, Chris, Alison, Nick, Hayley, Glynn, Bethan, Joyce, Claire and the many other teachers and friends who have encouraged me in the development of this material, contributed their own ideas and helped to proof read the contents of this book. This is for you too!

Dave Godfrey, December 2004

Introducing Dave Godfrey

Dave Godfrey is an experienced primary teacher, trainer, presenter, author and songwriter.

Dave taught throughout the Primary age-range during his teaching career in York and North Yorkshire. Dave has also worked as a teacher for the York Schools and Youth Trust (YOYO), a Christian Educational Charity.

Dave has been writing songs since 1998 and has produced the following albums:

(Photo © Andy Smith)

For the Christian Market:
Brave and Daring	(1999)	-	Christian Children's Songs
Heaven's No. 1	(2001)	-	Christian Children's Songs
Dependence Day	(2003)	-	Christian Children's Songs
An Audience of One	(2005)	-	Christian Children's Songs

For the Educational Market:
On the Shoulders of Giants	(2001)	-	Collective Worship Songs with Numeracy Links
Number Fun Song Resource Pack 1	(2003)	-	Songs to support KS1 & FS Numeracy Objectives
Number Fun Song Resource Pack 2	(2005)	-	More songs to support KS1 & FS Numeracy Objectives

(See page 52/53 for further details about these Educational resources)

Dave travels across the UK to present his material at Teacher Training events and on his special **'Key Stage 1 - Number Fun Activity Days'** in schools. Details of how to book Dave to come to your school can be found on page 54 of this resource.

"The children loved the Keep Fit Song best of all. It was great because it kept them all active and focused. Six year old Ben called it, "quality", and Tommy remarked, "Feel your heart beat!""
Lisa Threadgill, Y2 teacher

"We had a terrific Activity Day - children and adults alike. Many parents commented on the children's enjoyment and I even used two songs in a presentation to parents. The children have that special feeling, now they know the author!"
Deputy Head, Peterborough Primary School

"The children really enjoyed the lessons. The learning level and enjoyment was sky high! The Y5/6 special needs group enjoyed every minute, joined in enthusiastically and the songs were adapted to suit their level."
Maths Co-ordinator, Leeds Primary School

Contents

Page		Song		Theme
4		Introduction		
5		Numeracy Strategy Themes		

Songs

6	1	Cheeky Monkey's Counting Song	-	Counting Back from 10 to 0
8	2	Clap Snap	-	Equivalent Coin Values
10	3	Coins on the Floor	-	More Than
12	4	Farmer Pete's Chicken Song	-	Addition (& Subtraction) Problems
14	5	Funky Pictures	-	Addition / 1 more
16	6	Hiding in My Bag	-	2D and 3D Shapes
18	7	In a Week	-	Days in a Week
20	8	In the Biscuit Tin	-	Counting Back from 10 to 0
22	9	January, February	-	Ordering 12 Months
24	10	Little Soldiers	-	Counting On from 1 to 10
26	11	Mega Measurements	-	Standard Units of Measure
28	12	Mick the Mechanic	-	Partitioning
30	13	My Drink Survey	-	Pairs of Numbers to 100
32	14	My Football Team	-	Number Bonds to 10
34	15	Number Bond (006/004)	-	Number Bonds to 10
36	16	Number Fun Rocket	-	Counting Back
38	17	Perfect Pizza Parlour	-	Fractions
40	18	Safe in the Barn	-	Counting On from 0 to 10
42	19	The Adventures of Rover	-	2, 5 and 10 Times Tables
44	20	The Difference	-	Difference
46	21	The Keep Fit Song	-	Position Vocabulary
48	22	Tick Tock	-	Recognising Clock Times
50	CS	Celebration Song	-	Celebrating Achievement

| 52 | Number Fun Resources available from Omega Zone Publishing |
| 54 | Collective Worship Resources, Ordering and Number Fun Activity Days |

Key Stage 1 Number Fun

Introduction

Welcome to the second **'Key Stage 1 - Number Fun'** Song Resource Pack!

"Researchers have shown that music, can enhance student's abilities to access, interpret and retain learning content." (p165)
"When music is used explicitly to carry content, recall is easier." (p171)
     (Accelerated Learning in the Primary School' By Alistair Smith and Nicola Call, Network Ed Press, 1999)

As you can see from the quotes above, there is an increased awareness of the power of music to help children to learn. Music and Maths are a great combination - children can learn loads and have fun at the same time!

I hope you find the material enclosed in this pack very usable and a valuable support to your teaching of the National Numeracy Strategy.

The pack includes 22 songs to help you teach mathematics through the use of simple, engaging and fun songs. Each song aims to support the teaching of at least one objective from KS1 and FS stages of the National Numeracy Strategy. They are listed for you according to their themes on page 5.

There are three types of song in this pack:

- **Memory Songs** (e.g. January, February) These songs are designed to be memorised and practised regularly to help children learn key concepts and facts.
- **Interactive Songs** (e.g. Coins on the Floor) These songs are designed to help children practise a particular concept or skill. The teacher (or a child) is required to input a number or some information and the children then come up with answer to the problem within the structure of the song.
- **Celebration Song** I have included this bonus track to help you celebrate the work of your children. This song can be adapted and used across the Primary curriculum.

The following pages are full of kinaesthetic, visual and auditory ideas, designed to enable all your children to benefit from the songs, whatever their preferred learning styles. Each song comes with it's own presentation and prop ideas, as well as suggestions on how to adapt and extend the material.

All the songs are used during my 'Key Stage 1 - Number Fun Activity Days' and in a growing number of Primary schools across the country. You will find 2 CDs at the back of this book, one with all 23 'Key Stage 1 - Number Fun' songs on, and the other with backing tracks for all the songs. Each song has 2 dedicated pages within this book with all the information you will need to successfully use them in the classroom.

Please note that this is not a photocopyable resource, apart from the resource pages at the end of the book. Please do not make copies of the accompanying CDs, as this also breaks the copyright laws.

You will find downloadable resources and further ideas to support the use of these songs on the Number Fun website: www.numberfun.co.uk. Please do let us know of any good ideas you might come up with!

Finally, do share some of the songs with your KS2 colleagues, as many of them are very adaptable and have been successfully used in KS2, especially in Years 3 and 4.

Please let me know have you get on with these songs!
Have fun and enjoy your Mathematics!

Dave Godfrey

Dave Godfrey
Email: dave@numberfun.co.uk
Website: www.numberfun.co.uk

(Photo © Andy Smith)

Numeracy Strategy Themes

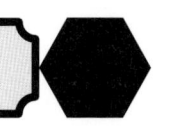

Each Numeracy based song has been written to help support the teaching of at least one objective from the National Numeracy Strategy. The song titles are recorded below in their themes.

Numbers and the Number System

Counting Songs	① Cheeky Monkey's Song	-	Counting Back from 10 to 0
	⑧ In the Biscuit Tin	-	Counting Back from 10 to 0
	⑩ Little Soldiers	-	Counting On from 1 to 10
	⑱ Safe in the Barn	-	Counting On from 0 to 10
Place Value and Ordering	③ Coins on the Floor	-	More Than
	⑫ Mick the Mechanic	-	Partitioning
	⑯ Number Fun Rocket	-	Counting Back
Fractions	⑰ Perfect Pizza Parlour	-	Fractions

Calculations and Solving Problems

Addition and Subtraction	④ Farmer Pete's Chicken Song	-	Addition Problems
	⑤ Funky Pictures	-	Addition / 1 more
	⑬ My Drink Survey	-	Pairs of Numbers to 100
	⑳ The Difference	-	Difference
Number Bonds	⑭ My Football Team	-	Number Bonds to 10
	⑮ Number Bond (006/004)	-	Number Bonds to 10
Money	② Clap Snap	-	Equivalent Coin Values
Multiplication Facts	⑲ The Adventures of Rover	-	Multiplication Facts

Measures, Shape and Space

Measuring Units	⑪ Mega Measurements	-	Standard Units of Measure
Position Vocabulary	㉑ The Keep Fit Song	-	Position Vocabulary
Shape	⑥ Hiding in My Bag	-	2D and 3D Shapes
Time	⑦ In a Week	-	Days in a Week
	⑨ January, February	-	Ordering 12 Months
	㉒ Tick Tock	-	Recognising Clock Times

Key Stage 1 – Number Fun

1 Cheeky Monkey's Counting Song

Numeracy Objective Link - Counting Back from 10 to 0

F Stage: **Say and use the number names in order in familiar contexts** such as number rhymes, songs, stories, counting games and activities (first to five, then ten, then twenty and beyond).

Find 1 more or one less than a number from 1 to 10.

Year 1: Know the number names and recite them in order to at least 20, from and back to zero.

Within the range 0-30, say the number that is 1 or 10 more or less than a given number.

Presentation and Prop Ideas

➢ Ask 10 children to play the part of the monkeys in the song. You may wish to put a big numbered sticker on each child to indicate which monkey they are or make a set of monkey masks with the numbers clearly marked on each one. Each child then pretends to swing in the tree, fall to the ground and, as appropriate, cry out, "Oh No!" and "Ow!"

➢ Purchase a set of monkey puppets or cuddly toys. The children can then hold these toys and act out the song as described in the idea above.

➢ Use the 'Cheeky Monkey's Counting Song' story-board from the 'Big Teacher Game-board Poster Pack 2' available from Omega Zone Publishing - see page 53.

➢ Purchase and use the 'Cheeky Monkey's Counting Song' file from the 'Number Fun Whiteboard Files' to help present this song. *(Details of this resource can be found on page 53.)*

Adaptations and Extensions

➢ Use the backing track version of the song and change the numbers of monkeys involved. For example start with 20 monkeys and count down to 10.

➢ Alternatively you could start with 20 monkeys and have 2 monkeys falling out of the tree in each verse. In this way you can count back to 0 from 20 in 2s.

➢ Change the 'monkey' for another animal of your choice!

Actions

The children will have great fun acting as monkeys. A teacher version is even funnier - a real winner in the assembly context!

Links

Counting back is also tackled in;
Song 8: In the Biscuit Tin
Song 16: Number Fun Rocket

From 'Song Resource Pack 1';
Song 6: Counting On (& Back)
Song 22: Wobbly Tooth

10 Cheeky Monkeys! *(Photo © Andy Smith)*

Key Stage 1 - Number Fun

Cheeky Monkey's Counting Song
(Counting Back from 10 to 0)

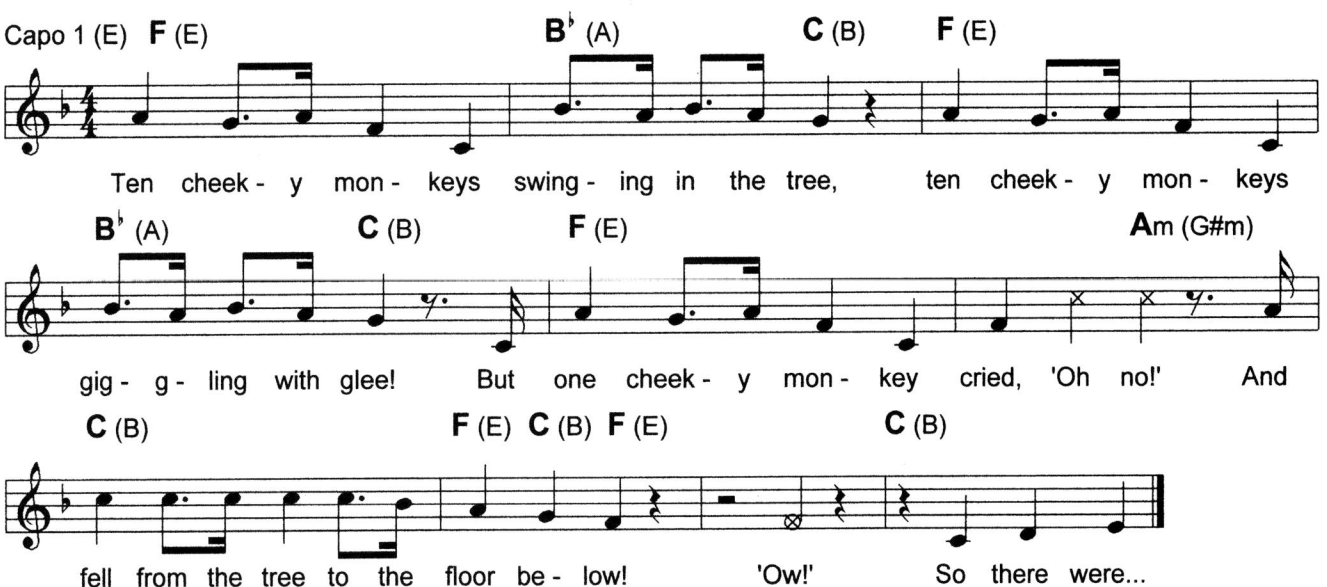

10 cheeky monkeys swinging in the tree,
10 cheeky monkeys giggling with glee!
But 1 cheeky monkey cried, "Oh no!",
And fell from the tree to the floor below!
"Ow!" So there were 9...

Etc...

1 cheeky monkey swinging in the tree,
1 cheeky monkey giggling with glee!
But 1 little monkey cried, "Oh no!",
And fell from the tree to the floor below!
"Ow!" So there were...

No cheeky monkeys swinging in the tree,
No cheeky monkey giggling with glee,
But 10 cheeky monkeys cried, "Wehey!"
And climbed up the tree once more that day!

© 2005 Dave Godfrey, Omega Zone Publishing
Please note: This is not a photocopyable resource

Key Stage 1 — Number Fun

Clap Snap

Numeracy Objective Link - Equivalent Coin Values

Year 1:   Recognise coins of different values.
          Work out how to pay an exact sum using smaller coins.
Year 2:   Recognise all coins.
          Find totals and work out which coins to pay.
Year 3:   Solve word problems involving money using one or more steps, including finding totals and working out which coins to pay.

Presentation and Prop Ideas

➤ Sit the children down on the carpet and hide some coins behind your back. As you go through the song, reveal the contents of each hand and the children should be encouraged to clap if the values are the same. Use with real coins or large cardboard versions.

➤ Prepare a set of flashcards with different combinations of coins, appropriate to the children's ability. As you sing the song, reveal two cards for the children to compare.

➤ Use the 'Sticky Toffee' big storyboard (Part of the 'Big Teacher Game-board Pack 1 - see page 53). Either have the story-board flat and use real coins, or vertical and use sticky-tack to secure the real or pretend coins to the story-board.

➤ Purchase and use the 'Sticky Toffee' file from the 'Number Fun Whiteboard Files' to help present this song. *(Details of this resource can be found on page 53.)*

Adaptations and Extensions

➤ You can adapt the song by varying the value of the coins which you use.

Actions

The children can hold out their left and right hands as you say, "Left" and "Right". The children also need to clap at the end of the song if the value of the coins are the same.

Links

The other song in this resource which supports the teaching of Money is;
   Song 3: Coins on the Floor *(See adaptation)*

From 'Song Resource Pack 1';
   Song 20: The Change

I can guarantee 'Clap Snap' helps you learn about money!
Miles, Y2

Key Stage 1 ✦ Number Fun

Clap Snap
(Equivalent Coin Values)

© 2005 Dave Godfrey, Omega Zone Publishing
Please note: This is not a photocopyable resource

This is Number Fun, Clap Snap,
Clapping when the value is the same.
This is Number Fun, Clap Snap,
Clapping when the value is the same.
To the left: (name coins),
To the right: (name coins),
This is Number Fun, Clap Snap,
Clap now if the value is the same!

Coins on the Floor

Numeracy Objective Link - More Than

F Stage: **Find one more than a number from 1 to 10.**

Year 1: **Within the range 0 to 30, say the number that is 1 or 10 more than any given number.**

Know by heart: addition facts for all pairs of numbers with a total up to at least 5.

Year 2: Say the number that is 1 or 10 more than any given two-digit number.

Know by heart: all addition facts for each number to at least 10.

Presentation and Prop Ideas

➢ Sit the children on the floor and sing the song whilst you, as the teacher, drop the appropriate number of coins on the floor.

➢ Split the children into pairs, giving each pair a number of coins. Sing the song to the backing track and allow one child from each pair to decide how many coins to drop. The other child has to answer to their partner. Great fun when everyone is playing in pairs at the same time!

Adaptations and Extensions

➢ Instead of using coins, use pens, rubbers or some other prop instead.

➢ Change the level of addition. Instead of adding 1 more, add 10 more or any other appropriate number for your children.

➢ Instead of counting the number of coins, have a go at calculating the value of the coins. You could change the lyrics of the last line to; How much money on the floor?

Actions

The children could pretend to drop the coins on the floor with you. You might like to make up a funky hand jive for the, 'Rattle, rattle, shake, shake' sections!

Links

'More than' and addition facts are also tackled in;
    Song 4: Farmer Pete's Chicken Song
    Song 5: Funky Pictures

From 'Song Resource Pack 1';
    Song 3: Bananas
    Song 12: It's My Birthday Today
    Song 14: My Name is Russ
    Song 19: The Change

Key Stage 1 Number Fun

Coins on the Floor
(More Than)

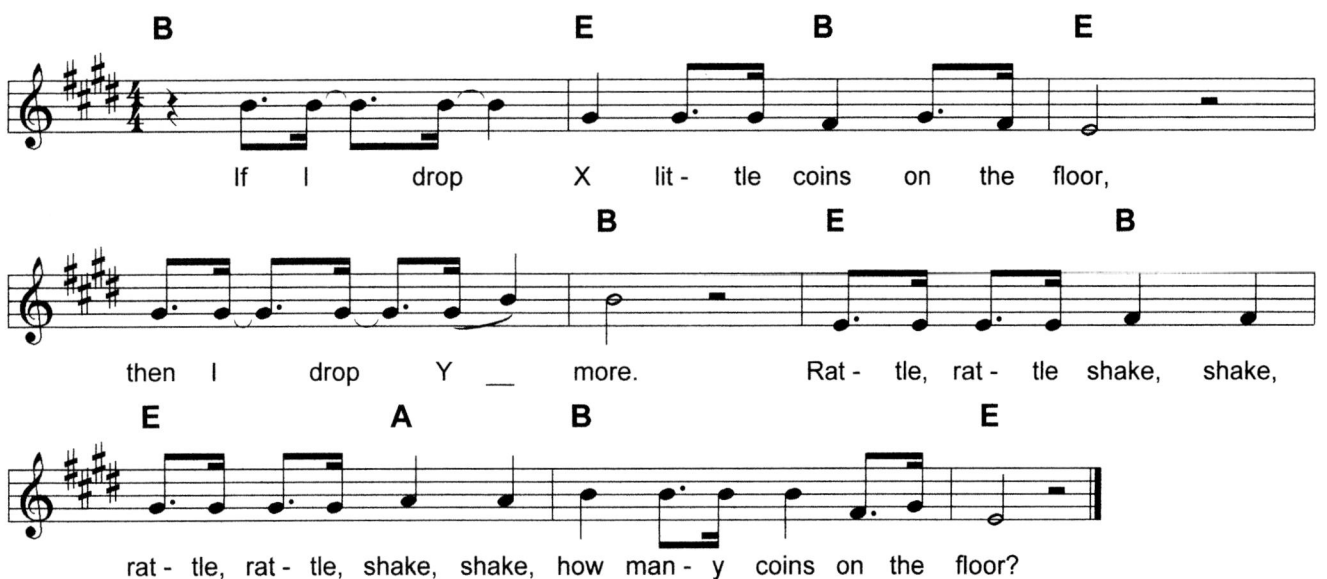

**If I drop X little* coins on the floor,
Then I drop Y more,
Rattle rattle shake shake,
Rattle rattle shake shake,
How many coins on the floor?**

© 2005 Dave Godfrey, Omega Zone Publishing
Please note: This is not a photocopyable resource

* Note: If the number X has more than two syllables, do not use this word.

4 — Farmer Pete's Chicken Song — 4

Numeracy Objective Link - Addition and Subtraction Problems

Year 1: **Use mental strategies to solve simple problems using counting, addition, subtraction etc.**

Year 2: Use known number facts and place value to add or subtract a pair of numbers mentally.

Presentation and Prop Ideas

➢ Have one of the children (or yourself) playing the part of Farmer Pete. Assign one part of the classroom to be the barn and another part to be the hen house. Use the children to be the chickens laying the eggs. Decide each time the number of eggs to be added together. As you sing the verse, the children move to the correct part of the room and deposit their egg! (This could be a pretend egg, or something representing an egg!) The whole class sings the song as they do so, making suitable chicken noises as they go!.

➢ Give the children the eggs as described above. Ask the 'chickens' to move and deposit their eggs in the location of their choice. Appoint two 'farm hands', one of which counts the eggs in the barn, and another to count the eggs in the hen house. These children then report back to Farmer Pete at the appropriate times in the song. As an adaptation of this idea, you could say to the 'chickens' that they do not need to lay an egg on every verse. The total would then fluctuate.

➢ Use the 'Farmer Pete's Chicken Song' Big storyboard from the 'Big Teacher Game-board Poster Pack 2'. (See page 53 for details). This will provide a great visual way of doing the song.

➢ Purchase and use the 'Farmer Pete's Chicken Song' file from the 'Number Fun Whiteboard Files' to help present this song. *(Details of this resource can be found on page 53.)*

Adaptations and Extensions

➢ Tackle Number Bonds by specifying, before you sing the song, that you know there are, e.g. 10 eggs on the farm this morning. However, you are not sure where they are! You could use 10 children to pretend to be the 10 chickens who laid the eggs. The children then move to the hen house or the barn as you sing the song.

➢ Adapt the song to tackle subtraction. Change the lyrics by swapping 'barn' and 'farm' in the last four lines so the song will read, 'X were on the farm, Y were in the hen house, How many in the barn?'

➢ Extend to adding 10, or adjusting to add 9 or 11.

Actions

The children will have great fun acting out the part of the chickens in the song!

Links

Addition and Subtraction facts are also tackled in;
    Song 3: Coins on the Floor
    Song 5: Funky Pictures

From 'Song Resource Pack 1';
    Song 3: Bananas
    Song 12: It's My Birthday Today
    Song 14: My Name is Russ
    Song 19: The Change

Great enjoyment!
M. Carr, Year 2 teacher

Key Stage 1 ★ Number Fun

Farmer Pete's Chicken Song
(Addition and Subtraction Problems)

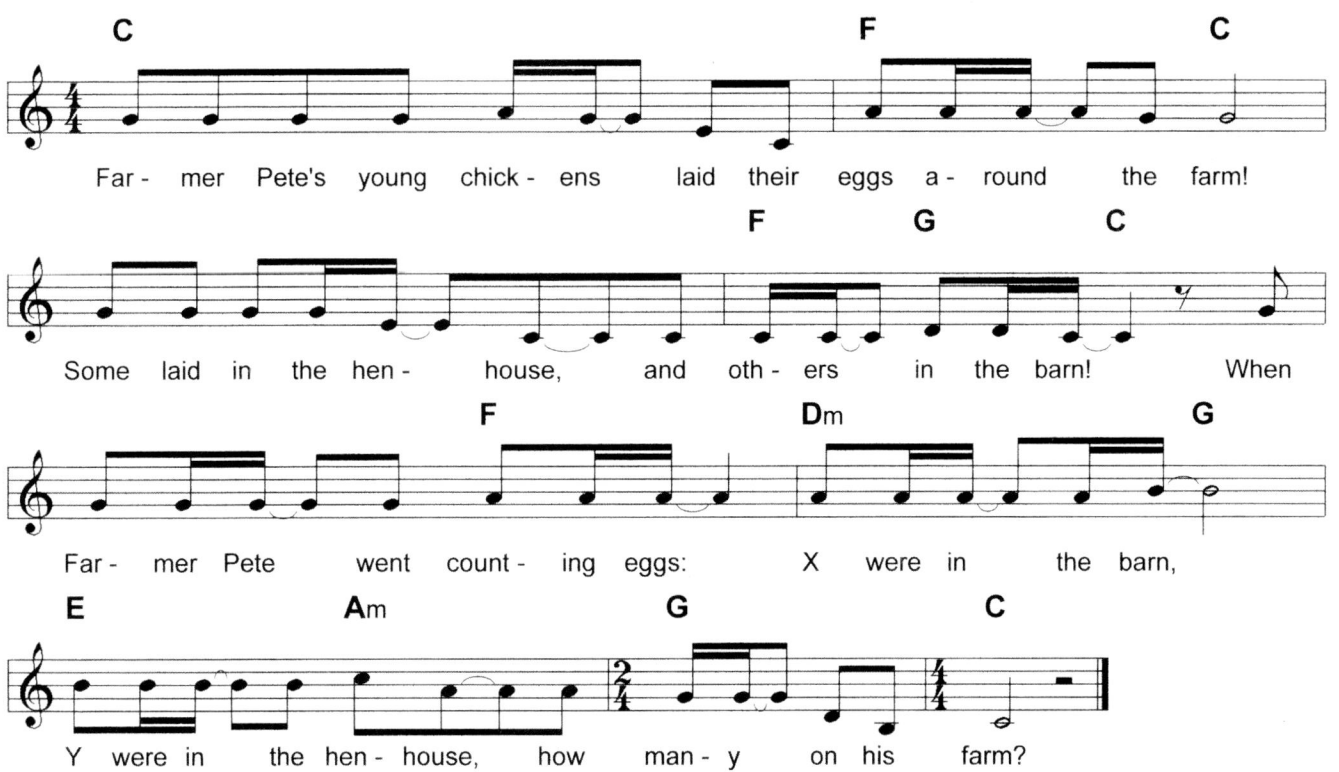

© 2005 Dave Godfrey, Omega Zone Publishing
Please note: This is not a photocopyable resource

(Sung)
Farmer Pete's young chickens
Laid their eggs around the farm!
Some laid in the hen house,
And others in the barn!
When Farmer Pete went counting eggs:
X were in the barn,
Y were in the hen house,
How many on his farm?

(Said)
I found (X+Y)!

Oliver is counting eggs! *(Photo © Andy Smith)*

Key Stage 1 — Number Fun

Funky Pictures

Numeracy Objective Link - Addition / 1 more

F Stage: **Find one more or one less than a number from 1 to 10.**
Begin to relate addition to combining two groups of objects, counting all the objects.

Year 1: **Know by heart:** addition facts for all pairs of numbers with a total up to at least 5.
Begin to know: addition facts for all pairs of numbers with a total up to at least 10.
Within the range 0 to 30, say the number that is 1 or 10 more or less than any given number.

Year 2: **Know by heart: all addition and subtraction facts for each number to at least 10.**
Say the number that is 1 or 10 more or less than any given two-digit number.

Presentation and Prop Ideas

➢ Sit the children down by the door to the classroom or another door which can safely be used. Have a pile of pictures on the floor which can then be stuck on the door. Sing the song using the pictures as a visual aid.

➢ Draw a picture of a door on your whiteboard. This would mean you could stick small pictures on to the board rather than using a real door. If you have an interactive whiteboard, you could easily manipulate pieces of clip art or pictures drawn by your children.

Adaptations and Extensions

➢ Adapt the level of the song by adding different numbers of pictures each time you sing the song.

➢ When working on shape, try substituting the words 'Funky Pictures' for 'circles' or 'red squares' etc.

Actions

The song is recorded to a funky, up-beat tempo. The children might like to make up a simple dance or hand-jive routine to accompany the song.

Links

Addition facts are also tackled in;
   Song 3: Coins on the Floor
   Song 4: Farmer Pete's Chicken Song

From 'Song Resource Pack 1';
   Song 3: Bananas
   Song 12: It's My Birthday Today
   Song 14: My Name is Russ
   Song 19: The Change

> Easy tune to learn. The children clapped the rhythm as they sang. Good reaction from the children first time we used it!
> M. Good, FS teacher

Key Stage 1 - Number Fun

Funky Pictures
(Addition / 1 more)

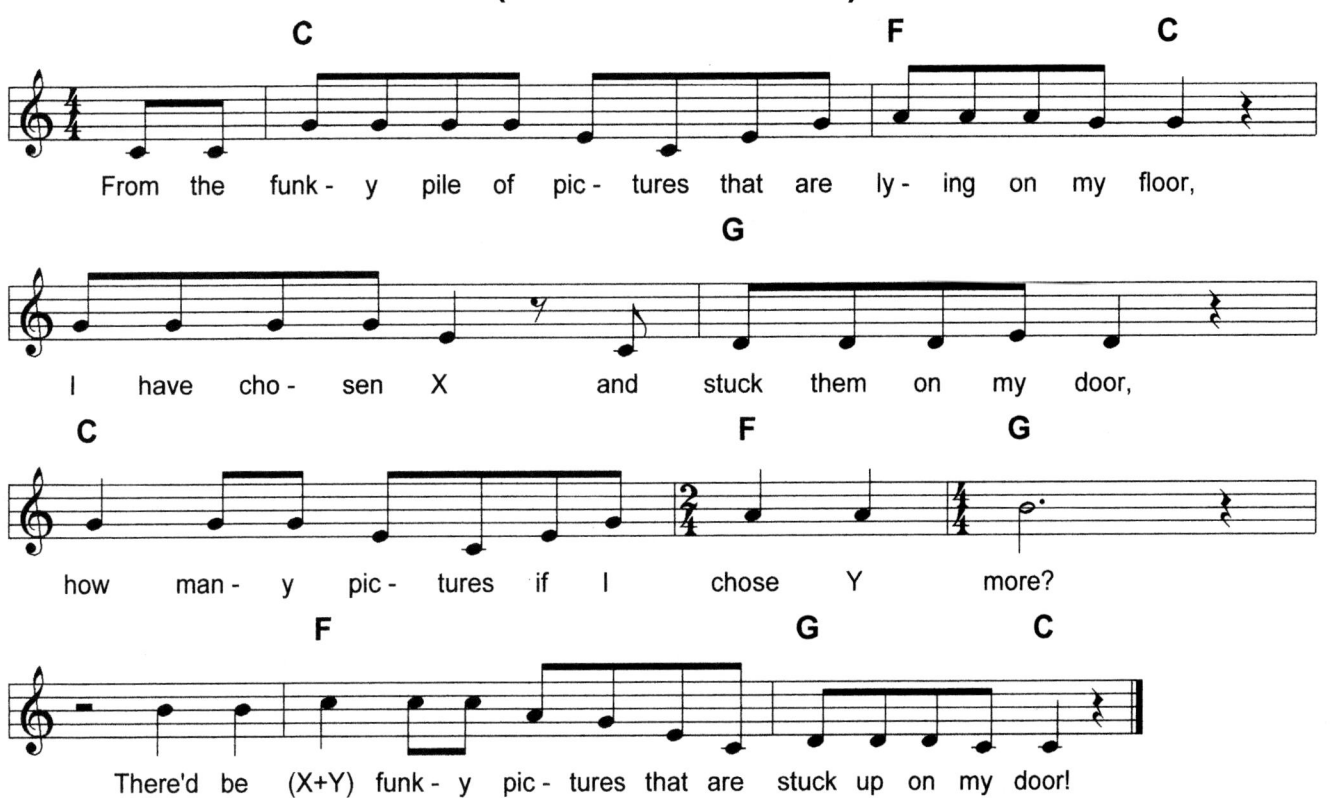

From the funky pile of pictures that are lying on my floor,
I have chosen X and stuck them on my door,
How many pictures if I chose Y more? ...
There'd be (X+Y) funky* pictures that are stuck upon my door!

© 2005 Dave Godfrey, Omega Zone Publishing
Please note: This is not a photocopyable resource

* Note: If the number (X + Y) has more than one syllable, do not use this word.

Key Stage 1 • Number Fun

6 Hiding in My Bag

Numeracy Objective Link - 2D and 3D Shapes

F. Stage: Use language such as 'circle' or 'bigger' to describe the shape and size of solids and flat shapes.
Year 1: Use everyday language to describe features of familiar 3D and 2D objects.
Year 2: Use the mathematical names for common 3D and 2D shapes; sort shapes and describe some of their features.

Presentation and Prop Ideas

➢ Make, or use an existing bag to hide a set of shapes in. Think of clear ways of describing each shape in the bag, which will fit with the song (see suggestions below). As you sing the song, choose one shape and reveal it at the appropriate moment.

➢ The children can play this game with each other using the backing track. Give each group of children a set of shapes and the song lyrics. The children have to guess what shape is being described by their friend.

➢ Make a set of flashcards which have the lyrics on one side and a picture of the chosen shape on the other. The children, using the visual and auditory clues, can then sing along to all the lyrics of the song and suggest the name of the shape.

Adaptations and Extensions

➢ Sing the song whilst all the children close their eyes and, concentrating really hard, try to visualise the shape being described.

➢ The list below contains some of the basic information for various shapes, including more complicated shapes. Children should be encouraged to identify more than one shape which has the properties you are describing. E.g. '4 corner, 4 sides, opposite sides the same' describes a square, rectangle and a rhombus!

➢ Ask the children to help you re-write the lyrics of the song. Give the children the name of a particular shape, or the shape itself, and ask them to suggest it's attributes. The children sing the sing the song to their friends.

Actions

As soon as the children recognise the shape, they can draw it in the air.

Links

This is the only song in this pack to tackle Shape. 'In Song Resource Pack 1' there is another shape song; Song 16: Shapes, which tackles 2D shapes.

2D Shapes

Equilateral Triangle: 3 corners - 3 sides - sides or corners the same.
Irregular Triangle: 3 corners - 3 sides - no sides the same.
Isosceles Triangle: 3 corners - 3 sides - 2 sides the same.

Square: 4 corners - 4 sides - sides the same.
Rectangle or Rhombus: 4 corners - 4 sides - opposite sides the same.
Quadrilateral: 4 corners - 4 sides.
Trapezium: 4 corners - 4 sides - 2 parallel sides.
Kite: 4 corners - 4 sides - 2 sides the same.

Regular Pentagon: 5 corners - 5 sides - sides the same.
Regular Hexagon: 6 corners - 6 sides - sides the same.

3D Shapes

Cube: 8 corners - 6 square faces - 12 edges - faces the same.
Cuboid: 8 corners - 6 rectangular faces - 12 edges - opposite faces the same.

Cylinder: 2 opposite identical circular faces - 1 curved face (rectangle).
Cone: 1 circular face - 1 point - put ice cream in here!

Square Based Pyramid: 8 edges - 5 faces - 5 corners.
Triangular Based Pyramid (Tetrahedron): 6 edges - 4 faces - 4 corners - triangular faces.

Key Stage 1 Number Fun

Hiding in My Bag
(2D and 3D Shapes)

There's a 2D (*or 3D*) shape hiding in my bag,
Can you guess its name?
There's a 2D (*or 3D*) shape hiding in my bag,
Oh can you guess its name?
It got X corners, Y sides!
Each side the same!
  (or 'No sides are the same!')
  (or 'Two sides are the same!')
  (or 'Opposites are the same!')
  (or 'Each face a square!' etc.)
There's a 2D (*or 3D*) shape hiding in my bag,
And Z is it's name!

© 2005 Dave Godfrey, Omega Zone Publishing
Please note: This is not a photocopyable resource

Key Stage 1 · Number Fun

In a Week

Numeracy Objective Link - Days in a Week

F Stage: Begin to know the days of the week in order.
Year 1: Know the days of the week.

Presentation and Prop Ideas

➢ Give the children a set of flashcards with the names of the days of the week marked on them. Ask the children to see if they can get themselves in chronological order. Teach the children the song and use the ordered children to help remember the words to the verse.

➢ Give all the children a flashcard with the name of one of the days written clearly on it. As with the first idea, the children should hold the flashcard when their day is mentioned.

➢ Play the 'Today Game' to reinforce a particular day of the week. Sing the song and every time you get to name of the day on which you are singing the song (e.g. Monday, if you are singing on Monday) ask the children to shout, clap or do something else. Naming the day then becomes a game which you can practice regularly!

➢ Start the song and ask the children to finish it off. Alternatively sing the song and deliberately get it wrong or miss something out and the children have to correct you.

Adaptations and Extensions

➢ The song is recorded with the traditional day of Sunday as the first day in the week. This might confuse the children a bit, as Monday is the beginning of the school week. You may wish to adapt the lyrics to take this into account.

Actions

The children can use their fingers to count the days of the week as you sing them. You can also add some appropriate clapping on the two beats after, 'In a Week', in the first and third lines of the song.

Links

Other songs which tackle Time are;
Song 9: January, February
Song 22: Tick Tock

From 'Song Resource Pack 1';
Song 1: 31 Days in January
Song 7: Counting Time
Song 21: The Story of My Day

> We use this song in the mornings to recall which day it is today!
> C Freeman, Y1 teacher

Key Stage 1 Number Fun

In a Week
(Days in a Week)

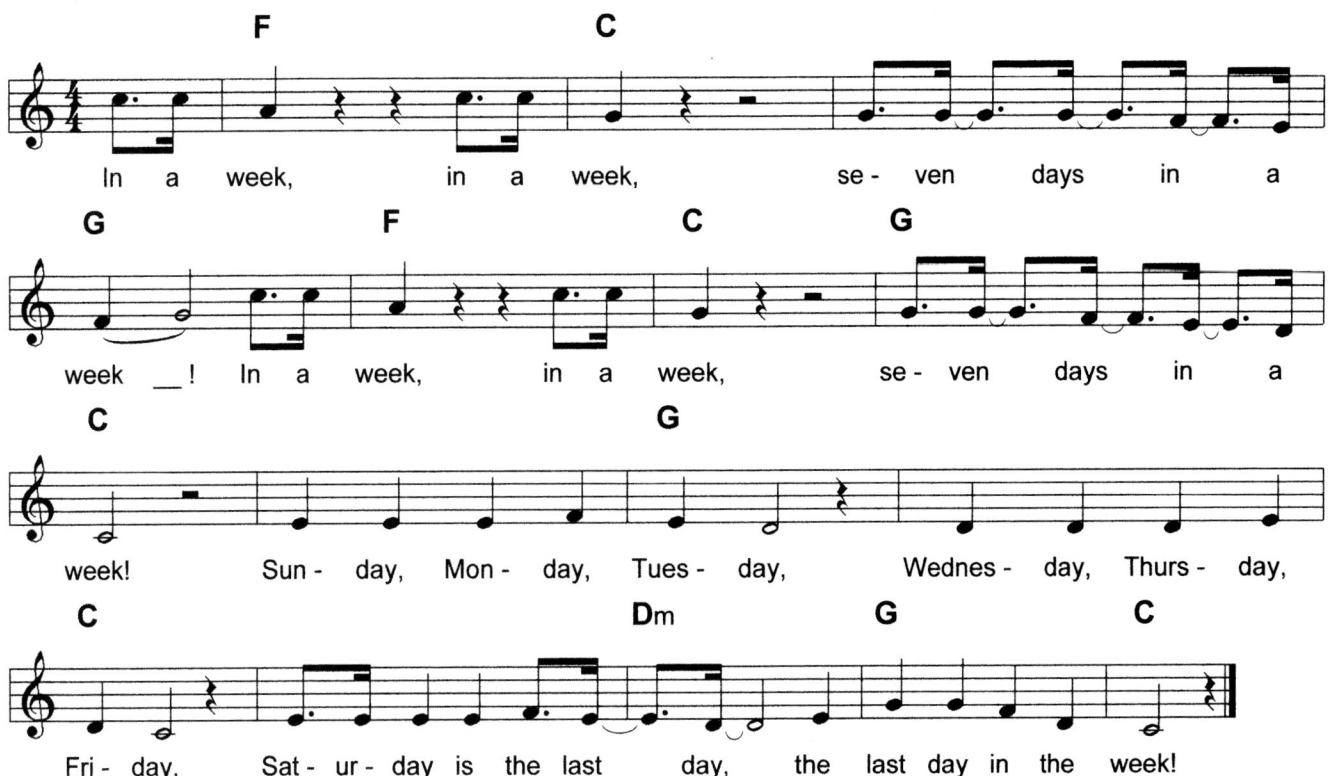

In a week, in a week,
7 days in a week!
In a week, in a week,
7 days in a week!

Sunday, Monday, Tuesday,
Wednesday, Thursday, Friday,
Saturday is the last day
The last day in the week!

In the Biscuit Tin

Numeracy Objective Link - Counting Back from 10 to 0

F Stage: **Say and use the number names in order in familiar contexts** such as number rhymes, songs, stories, counting games and activities (first to five, then ten, then twenty and beyond).

Find 1 more or one less than a number from 1 to 10.

Year 1: Know the number names and recite them in order to at least 20, from and back to zero.

Within the range 0-30, say the number that is 1 or 10 more or less than a given number.

Presentation and Prop Ideas

➢ Use pretend (or real!) biscuits and a large biscuit tin. Invite two or more children to the front and ask them to take turns in removing one biscuit from the biscuit tin at the end of each verse.

➢ Make a biscuit tin storyboard and a set of large laminated biscuits. Attach the biscuits to the storyboard using velcro or sticky tack. Remove them as you sing the song.

Adaptations and Extensions

➢ Change the lyrics of the song to: '2 little hands went diving in'. In this way you can count back in 2s.

➢ Change the lyrics of the song to: '5 little hands went diving in'. In this way you can count back in 5s!

➢ Start with 20 biscuits, or another number, and count back as appropriate.

Actions

The children can keep track of the number of biscuits still in the biscuit tin by using their fingers.

Links

Songs which tackle counting back from 10 include;
    Song 1: Cheeky Monkey's Counting Song
    Song 16: Number Fun Rocket

From 'Song Resource Pack 1';
    Song 6: Counting On (& Back)
    Song 22: Wobbly Tooth

A Custard Cream! *(Photo © Andy Smith)*

Key Stage 1 Number Fun

In the Biscuit Tin
(Counting Back from 10 to 0)

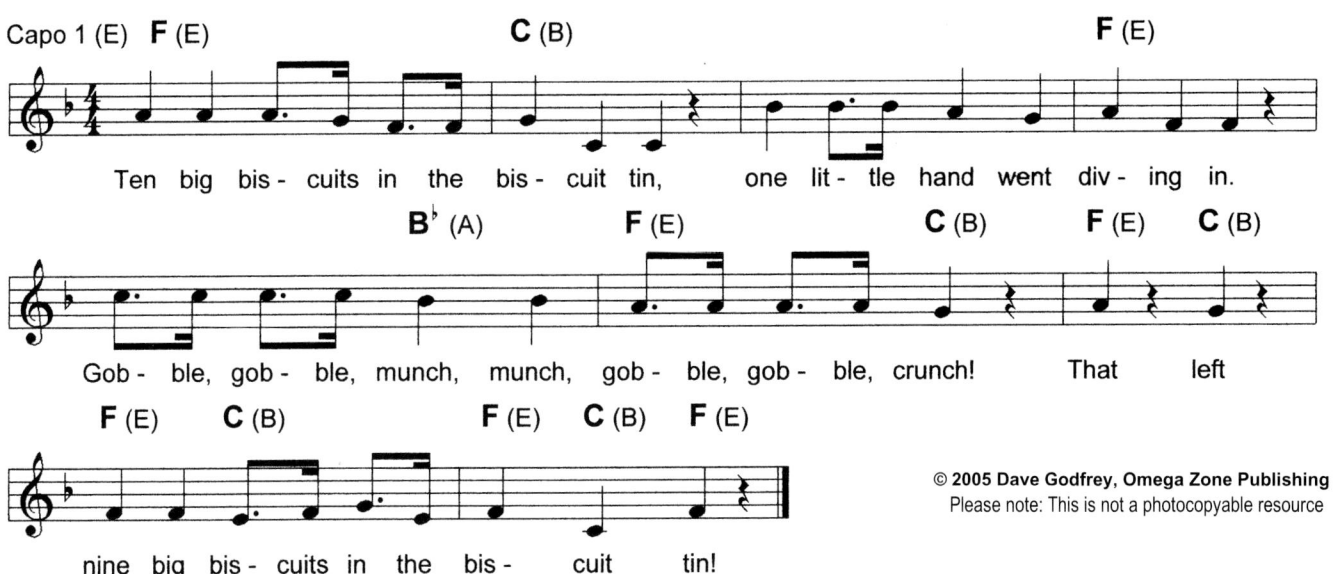

© 2005 Dave Godfrey, Omega Zone Publishing
Please note: This is not a photocopyable resource

**10 big biscuits in the biscuit tin,
1 little hand went diving in,
Gobble, gobble, munch, munch,
Gobble, gobble, crunch!
That left, 9 big biscuits in the biscuit tin! Etc...**

**1 big biscuit in the biscuit tin,
1 little hand went diving in,
Gobble, gobble, munch, munch,
Gobble, gobble, crunch!
That left, no big biscuits in the biscuit tin!**

**No big biscuits in the biscuit tin,
Then our Mum came walking in,
Gobble, gobble, munch, munch,
Gobble, gobble, crunch!
Now we're banned from biscuits in the biscuit tin!**

January, February

Numeracy Objective Link - Ordering 12 Months

Year 2: Order the months of the year.
Year 3: Use a calendar.

Presentation and Prop Ideas

- Make a set of flashcards with each one displaying the name of a different month. Give 12 children one flashcard each. Ask the children to complete the 'Ordering Challenge' to see if they can get themselves in the chronological order in less than 30 seconds. Once the children are in the correct order introduce the song as a way of remembering the order of the months. The flashcards will help them to remember the song.

- Make a set of flashcards which have a suitable picture or a number on them as another visual clue for the children as they try to remember the order.

- As you sing the song, ask the children to stand up when their birthday month is mentioned.

Adaptations and Extensions

- Use the children's birthdays as another way of remembering the order of the months. You could produce posters or flashcards with the names of the month and the children whose birthday falls within that month.

- Move onto discussing how many days there are in each month. A good way of doing this would be to use Song 1: 31 Days in January, from the first Song Resource Pack. Alternatively you could clearly mark the number of days within each month on each of the visuals that you use.

- Display the class calendar. Discuss the date each day.

Actions

There are no particular actions to this song suggested.

Links

Other songs which tackle Time are;
    Song 7: In a Week
    Song 22: Tick Tock

From 'Song Resource Pack 1';
    Song 1: 31 Days in January
    Song 7: Counting Time
    Song 21: The Story of My Day

> My children saw the older children sing this one and they requested it. Now they know the months in order!
> C Freeman, Y1 teacher

Key Stage 1 Number Fun

January, February
(Ordering 12 Months)

Jan-u-ar-y, Feb-ru-ar-y, March, A-pril and May,
June and Ju-ly, Aug-ust Sep-tem-ber, Oct-o-ber and No-vem-ber,
De-cem-ber is the last month in the year!
Full of joy and Christ-mas cheer, twelve months come and twelve months go, twelve months start a-gain I know, it's...
cem-ber is the last month!

© 2005 Dave Godfrey, Omega Zone Publishing
Please note: This is not a photocopyable resource

**January, February,
March, April and May,
June and July, August, September
October and November,
December is the last month in the year!
Full of joy and Christmas cheer.
12 months come and, 12 months go,
12 months start again, I know it's ...**

Little Soldiers

Numeracy Objective Link - Counting On from 1 to 10

F Stage: **Say and use the number names in order in familiar contexts** such as number rhymes, songs, stories, counting games and activities (first to five, then ten, then twenty and beyond).

Find 1 more or one less than a number from 1 to 10.

Year 1: Know the number names and recite them in order to at least 20, from and back to zero.

Within the range 0-30, say the number that is 1 or 10 more or less than a given number.

Presentation and Prop Ideas

➢ Ask 1 child to come to the front to be the first soldier. At the end of each verse the child chooses another child to come and join in the presentation. Eventually you will have a set of 10 strapping young soldiers at the front of the class!

➢ Choose 10 children and clearly mark, using a label, hat or a badge, what number soldier each child is representing. Sit the children down in a line. At the end of each verse the next child stands and joins the other soldiers who are exercising!

Adaptations and Extensions

➢ Instead of starting with one soldier, begin with another number and the class counts on from there.

➢ Count backwards using the following lyrics: '10 little soldiers exercising, 10 little soldiers bending up and down, 1 little soldier needs a rest, so he sits on the ground.'

➢ Instead of calling in one soldier at the end of each verse, call in 2 or 3 or a random number of soldiers as appropriate!

Actions

1 little soldier exercising,

(Soldiers stretch arms up and down, and then forwards and back, in time with the beat)

1 little soldier bending up and down,

(Soldiers bend up and down at the knees)

1 little soldier needs a friend so,

(Solders march on the spot)

Call in number 2!

(The last soldier to be called up, calls up the next one. The rest keep marching!)

Links

Counting On to 10 is also tackled in;
Song 3: Coins on the Floor
Song 18: Safe in the Barn

From 'Song Resource Pack 1';
Song 8: Dancing in the Sun
Song 11: I Can Count (& Spider)

(Photo © Andy Smith)

Little Soldiers

(Counting On from 0 to 10)

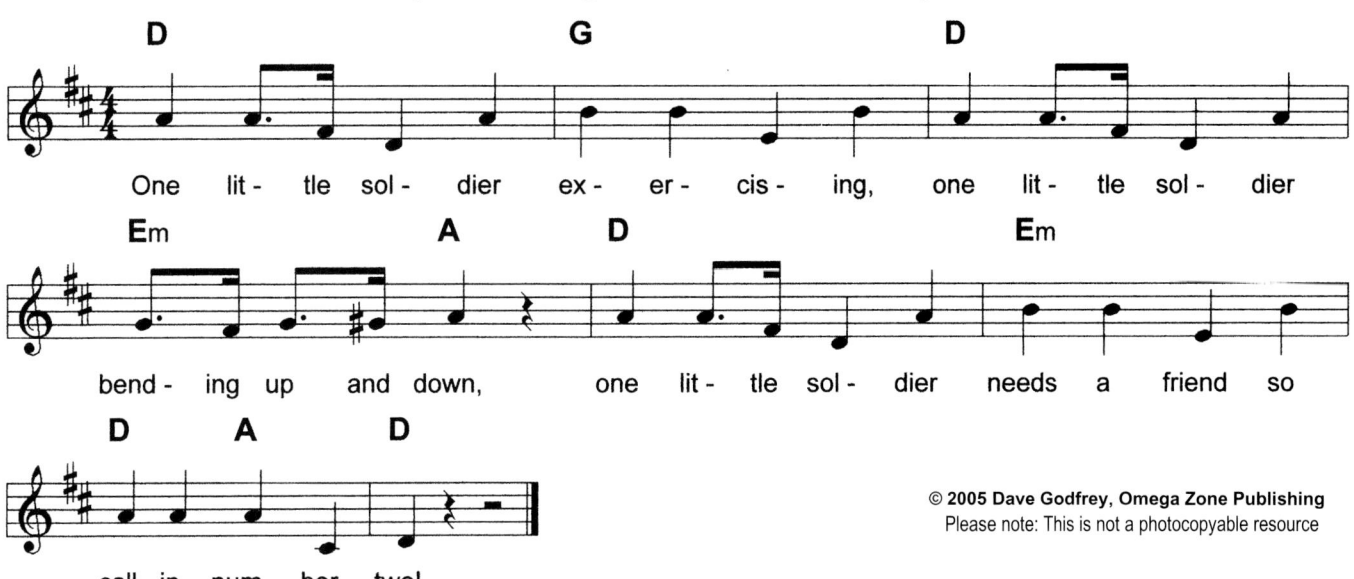

One little soldier exercising, one little soldier bending up and down, one little soldier needs a friend so call in number two!

© 2005 Dave Godfrey, Omega Zone Publishing
Please note: This is not a photocopyable resource

1 little soldier exercising,
1 little soldier bending up and down,
1 little soldier needs a friend so,
Call in number 2! Etc...

10 little soldier exercising,
10 little soldier bending up and down,
10 little soldier needs a friend so,
But no-one can be found!

<u>Final Verse</u>

10 little soldiers doing exercises,
10 little soldiers bending up and down,
10 little soldiers need a rest so,
So all sit on the ground!

Mega Measurements

Numeracy Objective Link - Standard Units of Measure

Year 1: **Suggest suitable standard or uniform non-standard units... then measure, a length, mass or capacity.**

Year 2: **Estimate, measure and compare lengths, masses and capacities, using standard units; suggest suitable units and equipment for such measurements.**

Year 3: Measure and compare using standard units.
Know the relationships between kilometres and metres, metres and centimetres, kilograms and grams, litres and millilitres.

Presentation and Prop Ideas

➢ The song is recorded on the CD as if sung by 2 old ladies. You could get two children to dress up as old ladies and ask them to hold a set of props! This will add a good level of comedy to the learning! Encourage the children to act out the song as it is sung by the class to the CD.

The props could include:

✓ Wigs and flowery dresses for the 'old ladies' to wear.
✓ A metre stick (or long tape measure), a kilogram weight and a litre jug.
✓ A 1 gram weight and something to represent a millimetre and millilitre.
✓ A biscuit tin full of cookies (either imagine the tin is full of cookies or use plastic ones!)
✓ 2 cups of Horlicks!

Adaptations and Extensions

➢ Rewrite the lyrics of the song. The song is recorded in the style of two old ladies. Why not try and write some versions for children, teenagers, parents or teachers?!

➢ Ask the children if Gladys and Vera should have chosen more appropriate units of measure. For example, they could have measured their height in centimetres, their cookies in grams and their Horlicks in millilitres!

Actions

Encourage the 'old ladies' to act out the song, using the props as suggested above!

Links

Measurement units are also tackled in;
Song 15: Pirate Captain Hugh (from 'Song Resource Pack 1')

Vera and Gladys enjoying their Horlicks!
(Photo © Andy Smith)

Key Stage 1 Number Fun

Mega Measurements
(Standard Units of Measure)

[Sheet music with chords: Capo 1 (E), F (E), C (B), Gm (F#m)]

Lyrics under the music:
One thou-sand mil-li-me-tres in a me-tre, one thou-sand lit-tle grams in a ki-lo-gram, one thou-sand mil-li-li-tres in a li-tre, it's true! Me-ga mea-sure-ments for me and you! We mea-sure our height in me-tres, we mea-sure our cook-ies in ki-lo-grams, we drink our Hor-licks in li-tres, it's true! Me-ga mea-sure-ments for me and you!

© 2005 Dave Godfrey, Omega Zone Publishing
Please note: This is not a photocopyable resource

**1 thousand millimetres in a metre,
1 thousand little grams in a kilogram,
1 thousand millilitres in a litre - it's true!
Mega measurements for me and you!**

**We measure our height in metres,
We measure our cookies in kilograms,
We drink our Horlicks in litres, it's true!
Mega measurements for me and you!**

Key Stage 1 Number Fun

Mick the Mechanic

Numeracy Objective Link - Partitioning

Year 1: Begin to know what each digit in a two-digit number represents. Partition a 'teens' number and begin to partition larger two-digit numbers into a multiple of 10 and ones (TU).

Year 2: **Know what each digit in a two-digit number represents, including 0 as a place holder**, and partition two-digit numbers into a multiple of tens and ones (TU).

Presentation and Prop Ideas

➢ Present the song using a simple set of actions similar to the set below.

➢ Dress one of the children up as 'Mick the Mechanic' and give them a 2 digit number. When you sing the song, they have the challenge of putting the number in their 'tool box' and bringing out two new cards to represent how that number is partitioned.

➢ Have a set of 'Place Value Arrow Cards' (or 'Digit Cards') which can be easily manipulated at the appropriate moment in the song to show the partitioning of each number.

Adaptations and Extensions

➢ For those children who would like a big challenge change the number so you they can partition between the hundreds and tens.

➢ Instead of singing about two different numbers during each verse of the song, repeat the first number to consolidate the partitioning.

Actions

Here are a set of simple actions you could use to sing the song!

I'm Mick the Mechanic, Mick the Mechanic,

(Pretend to be twist a tricky nut using a massive spanner.)

And I love to take numbers apart.

(Separate the joint and the spanner on the word, 'apart'.)

I'm Mick the Mechanic, Mick the Mechanic,

And I love to take numbers apart.

(Repeat as above)

Like AB is A tens and B units, and CD is C tens and D units.

(Use some easy to manipulate digit cards to show the partitioning in action.)

Links

This is the only song from both Song Resource Packs which tackles the topic of Partitioning.

A fantastic way to introduce the difficult topic of partitioning.
G Robinson, Y1 teacher

Key Stage 1 Number Fun

Mick the Mechanic
(Partitioning)

I'm Mick the Mechanic, Mick the Mechanic, I love to take numbers apart. I'm Mick the Mechanic, Mick the Mechanic, I love to take numbers apart. Like AB is A tens and B units, CD is C tens and D units.

© 2005 Dave Godfrey, Omega Zone Publishing
Please note: This is not a photocopyable resource

I'm Mick the Mechanic,
Mick the Mechanic,
And I love to take numbers apart.
I'm Mick the Mechanic,
Mick the Mechanic,
And I love to take numbers apart.
Like AB is A tens and B units,
And CD is C tens and D units.

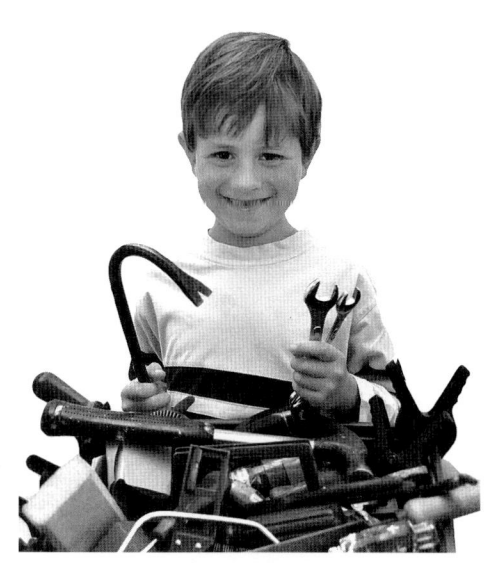

Mick the Mechanic, hard at work! *(Photo © Andy Smith)*

Key Stage 1 — Number Fun

My Drinks Survey

Numeracy Objective Link - Pairs of Numbers to 100

Year 2: Know by heart: all pairs of multiples of 10 with a total of 100 (e.g. 30 + 70).

Year 3: Derive quickly: all pairs of multiples of 5 with a total of 100 (e.g. 35 + 65).

Presentation and Prop Ideas

➢ Make 10 posters or flashcards with each one representing 10 teachers. Make another 2 signs or posters which are clearly marked 'tea' and 'coffee'. Ask 10 children to hold a teacher flashcard and pin the drinks posters on two sides of the classroom. As you sing the song the children with the posters move to the appropriate side of the classroom.

➢ Make a story-board to help you present the song. Again you could have 10 small pictures of 10 teachers and two big 'mugs' to represent the drinks. By placing the 'teachers' on the 'mugs' you can represent the values you wish to use within the song.

Adaptations and Extensions

➢ You could change the number of teachers involved in the survey. You could try the song with 10, 20 or 1000 teachers!

➢ Sing the song using pairs of numbers which are multiples of 5 and have the total of 100.

➢ Use the song as a basis for a data handling lesson. Produce a graph from one of the verses of the song. Use your own graph and ask the children to interpret the numbers.

Actions

The children could use their fingers to work out the answers within each verse. Equally they might like to pretend to eat the cake and have a refreshing drink!

Links

This is the only song from both Song Resource Packs which is specifically written to practice pairs of numbers to 100.

The Drinks Survey in action! *(Photo © Andy Smith)*

Key Stage 1 Number Fun

My Drinks Survey
(Pairs of Numbers to 100)

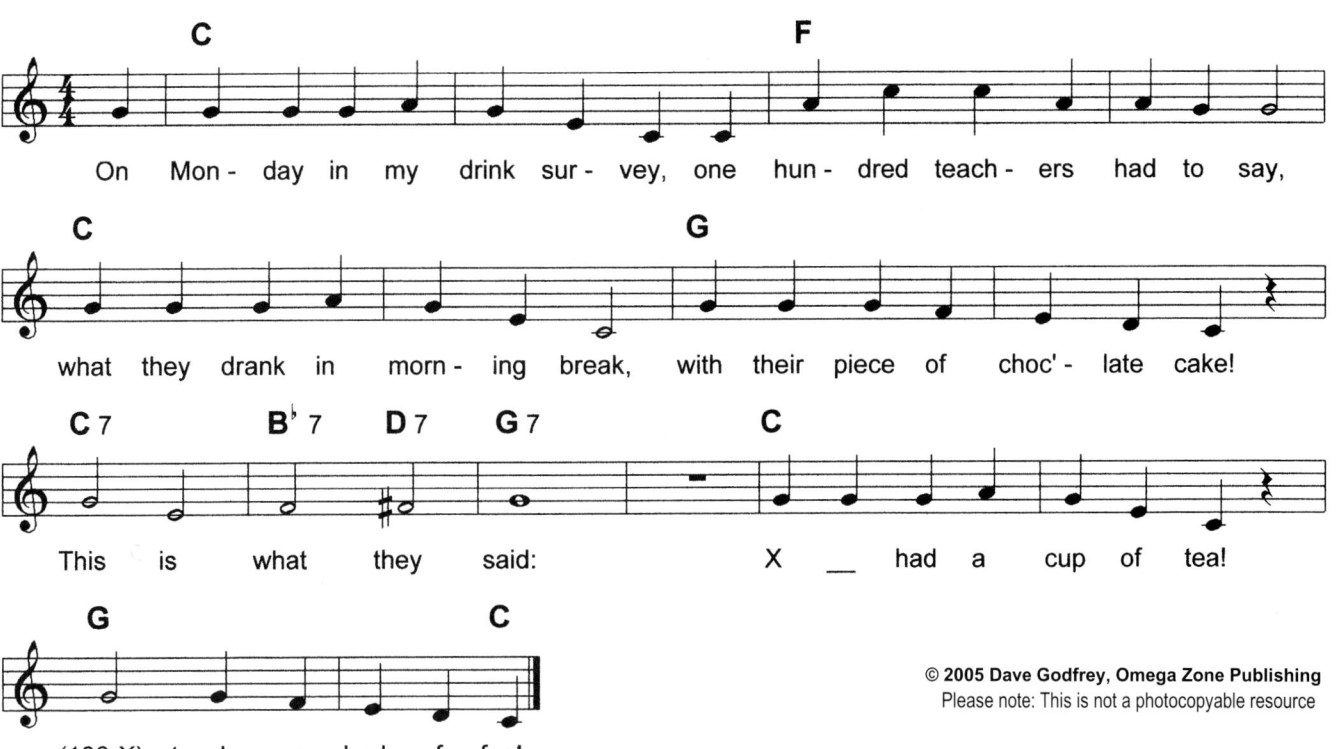

On Monday* in my drink survey,
One hundred teachers had to say,
What they drank in morning break,
With their piece of chocolate cake!
This is what they said:
X had a cup of tea!
(100 - X) teachers had coffee!

© 2005 Dave Godfrey, Omega Zone Publishing
Please note: This is not a photocopyable resource

* Note: Song is recorded with 5 verses, using the days; Monday to Friday.

Key Stage 1 Number Fun

My Football Team

Numeracy Objective Link - Number Bonds

F. Stage: **Begin to relate addition to combining two groups of objects, and subtraction as 'taking away'.**

Year 1: **Know by heart all pairs of numbers with a total of 10.**

Year 2: **Know by heart all pairs of numbers with a total of 20.**

Presentation and Prop Ideas

➤ Use a set of small football figures to represent the footballers in the song. Dress the leader of the song (which could be you or a child) in a football top and then hide the football figures behind you in your hands. At the appropriate moment show the number of players you have already got by revealing that number of figures in your right hand. Then show the figures in the left hand at the end of each verse to confirm to the children that they have answered correctly.

➤ Ask the children to design and make a storyboard of a football pitch with removable players. Use the story-board as a visual illustration of the song.

➤ Dress up 11 of the children in the school football kit. Make sure the Captain is distinctive because he is not counted within the 10 other players used to represent the number bond. The children then move to represent the numbers in the song.

Adaptations and Extensions

➤ It is relatively easy to change the number bond tackled by the song. The cup final could be a 5 a-side, 7a-side or even a 12 a-side affair.

➤ You could also change the sport and tackle number bonds to 14 and 15 by pretending to be rugby teams!

Actions

The children might like to make up a 'warm-up' dance routine which mirrors some of the simple stretches which footballers tend to do before a football match.

Point to the 'captain' when you sing 'I'm the captain'.

Children can shout out the lines, 'Win the cup!' and 'We will win!'

Links

Number Bonds to 10 are also tackled in;
Song 15: Number Bond (006/004)

From 'Song Resource Pack 1';
Song 10: Farmer Pete
Song 17: Sticky Toffees

My Year Two children loved dressing up in the school's football shirts to act out this championship winning song!
M Carr, Year 2 teacher

Key Stage 1 Number Fun

My Football Team
(Number Bonds to 10)

I'm the captain of my football team,
I need 10 players to help me win the cup!
I got X players, I need to score,
It's not enough - 'cos I need (10 - X) more!
And with these players in my football team,
WE WILL WIN!

© 2005 Dave Godfrey, Omega Zone Publishing
Please note: This is not a photocopyable resource

Celebrating a famous victory!
(Photo © Andy Smith)

Key Stage 1 · Number Fun

Number Bond (006/004)

Numeracy Objective Link - Number Bonds

F. Stage: **Begin to relate addition to combining two groups of objects, and subtraction as 'taking away'.**

Year 1: **Know by heart all pairs of numbers with a total of 10.**

Year 2: **Know by heart all pairs of numbers with a total of 20.**

Presentation and Prop Ideas

➤ This song is a take off of 'James Bond - 007'! Use eleven children; one child representing Number Bond and 10 children representing the 'Sneaky Ten'. Dress Number Bond up smartly to look like a secret agent, and dress the 'Sneaky Ten' to look like criminals (they could all wear sunglasses!). Assign one area of the room to Number Bond as his special police cell, into which he can put the criminals that he will find hiding around the classroom once the song starts. The children who are not acting need to help Number Bond to sing the song. The 10 criminals need to come 'fair and square' into the police cell once they are spotted by Number Bond. There is lots of opportunity for fun during this presentation and a host of discussion points that can come from it!

➤ Use the 'Number Bond (006/004)' big story-board from the 'Big Teacher Game-board Poster Pack Set 2', details of which are on page 53. The story-board has the story set in 'Shape City' and provides an excellent visual way of presenting the song. The story-board is designed to help you discuss 2D and 3D shapes too!

➤ Purchase and use the 'Number Bond (006/004)' file from the 'Number Fun Whiteboard Files' to help present this song. *(Details of this resource can be found on page 53.)*

Adaptations and Extensions

➤ Instead of running the story from the beginning to end, as recorded on the CD, try mixing the verses up! You could pretend that some of the criminals manage to escape from the prison or Number Bond has managed to capture more than one criminal at a time!

➤ You can extend the learning to other parts of the curriculum by using the song as a basis for creative writing. The children could pretend to be Number Bond or be one of the 'Sneaky Ten'.

Actions

When acting out the story and song you should encourage the children to really act out the part. The other children could pretend to be ordinary folk from 'Shape City'.

Links

Number Bonds to 10 are also tackled in;
    Song 14: My Football Team

From 'Song Resource Pack 1';
    Song 10: Farmer Pete
    Song 17: Sticky Toffees

Oh No! Not the famous 006/004!
(Photo © Andy Smith)

Number Bond (006/004)
(Number Bonds to 10)

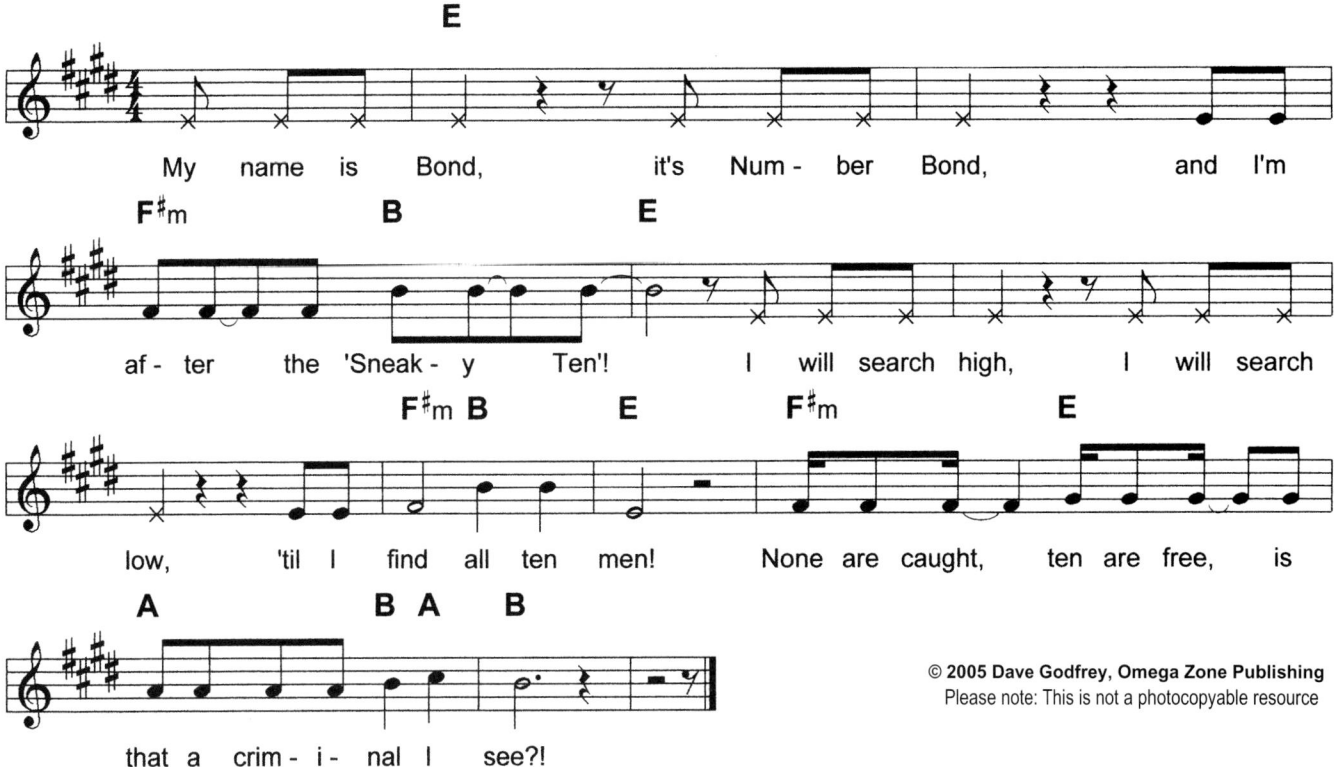

© 2005 Dave Godfrey, Omega Zone Publishing
Please note: This is not a photocopyable resource

**My name is Bond, it's Number Bond,
And I'm after the 'Sneaky Ten'!
I will search high, I will search low,
'Till I find all ten men!
None are caught, 10 are free, is that a criminal I see?! Etc...**

**My name is Bond, it's Number Bond,
And I've caught three out of ten.
I will search high, I will search low,
'Till I find the last seven men!
3 are caught, 7 are free, is that a criminal I see?! Etc...**

**My name is Bond, it's Number Bond,
And I've caught you 'Sneaky Ten'!
I did search high, I did search low,
Now don't escape again!**

Key Stage 1 ✱ Number Fun

Number Fun Rocket

Numeracy Objective Link - Counting Back

F. Stage: Recite the number names in order, continuing the count forwards or backwards from a given number.

Year 1: Count on and back in ones from any small number, and in tens from and back to zero.

Year 2: **Count on and back in ones and tens from any two-digit number.**

Presentation and Prop Ideas

➢ Sit the children on the floor in the shape of a rocket. Have a row of 11 children who are the 'spine' of the rocket. Sing the song with the 11 children on the spine being responsible for standing up at the appropriate point in the song and singing out the countdown. These children could also have a flashcard in their hands to represent the number they are to sing out. All the children could sing along with the 'spine' as they stand and show their flashcards.

➢ Use the 'Number Fun Rocket' big story-board from the 'Big Teacher Game-board Poster Pack Set 2', details of which are on page 53. The story-board has a big rocket on it and three sets of numbers to represent different types of countdown. Place the required countdown up the spine of the rocket as a visual representation.

➢ Purchase and use the 'Number Fun Rocket' file from the 'Number Fun Whiteboard Files' to help present this song. *(Details of this resource can be found on page 53.)*

Adaptations and Extensions

➢ The song is flexible enough to cope with any countdown! Stretch the children by doing unusual countdowns. For example, you could try a negative number countdown!

➢ If you are using the 'Number Fun Rocket' big story-board as a laminated poster, you can use it as a write on/wipe off board. This will then allow you to have a play with each countdown. You could miss some numbers out or have a crazy pattern which the children have to guess before the countdown takes place.

➢ Change the lyrics to turn 'Number Fun Rocket' into a counting on song.

> *Number Fun Rocket, heading to the moon,*
> *Number Fun Rocket, getting there soon,*
> *Count miles in 2s,*
> *Starting at zero,*
> *Here we go...*

Actions

The children could use their fingers to represent the countdown. The could also stand and do some physical movements to the countdown. For example, '10: twist right, 9: twist left, 8: twist left again...' etc.

Links

Counting back is also tackled in;
 Song 1: Cheeky Monkey's Counting Song
 Song 8: In the Biscuit Tin

From 'Song Resource Pack 1';
 Song 6: Counting On (& Back)
 Song 22: Wobbly Tooth

Number Fun Rocket
(Counting Back)

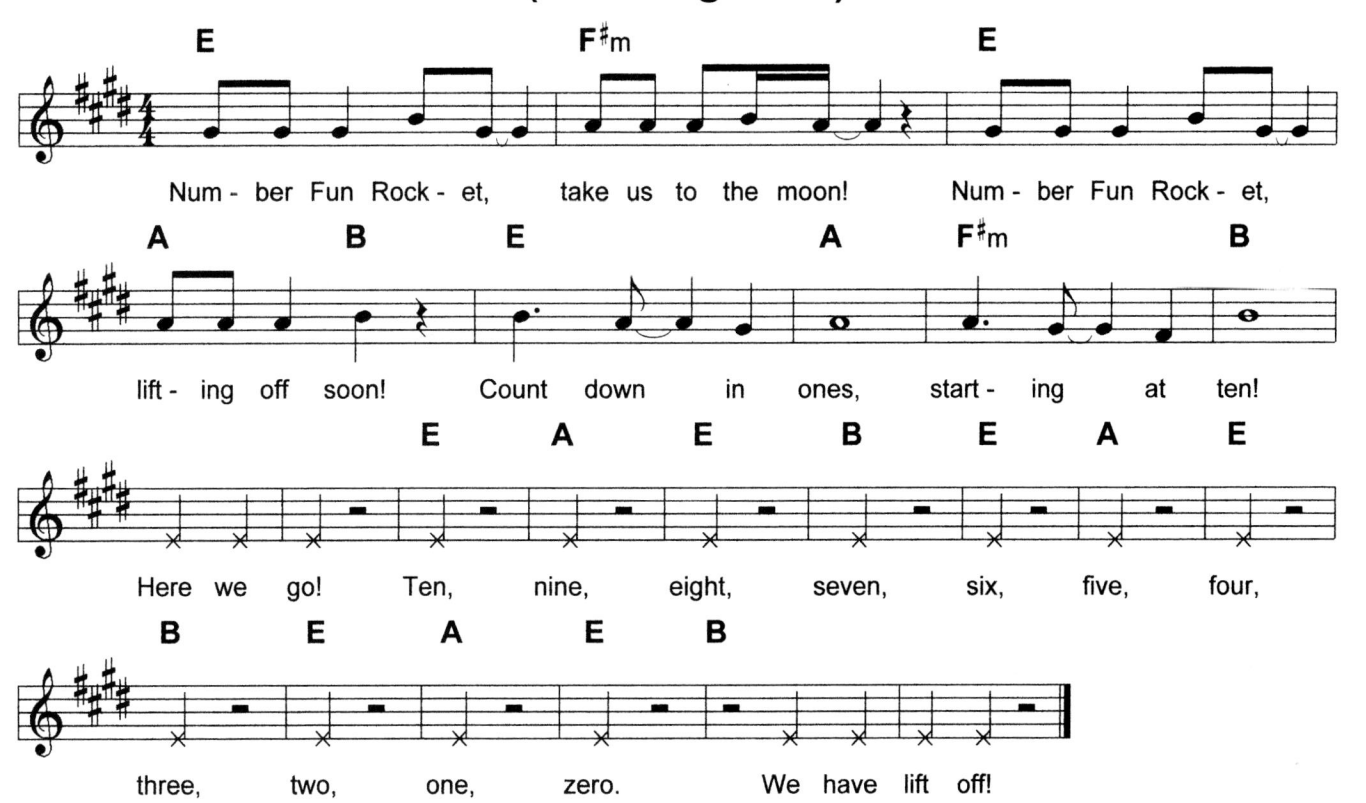

Num-ber Fun Rock-et, take us to the moon!
Num-ber Fun Rock-et, lift-ing off soon!
Count down in ones, start-ing at ten!
Here we go! Ten, nine, eight, seven, six, five, four,
three, two, one, zero. We have lift off!

© 2005 Dave Godfrey, Omega Zone Publishing
Please note: This is not a photocopyable resource

Number Fun Rocket, take us to the moon!
Number Fun Rocket, lifting off soon!
Count down in 1's,
Starting at 10!
Here we go!
10, 9, 8, 7, 6, 5, 4, 3, 2, 1, 0.
We have lift off!

Count down in 10's,
Starting at 100! ... 100, 90, 80, 70, 60, 50, 40, 30, 20, 10, 0.

Count down in 2's,
Starting at 20! ... 20, 18, 16, 14, 12, 10, 8, 6, 4, 2, 0.

Count down in 5's,
Starting at 50! ... 50, 45, 40, 35, 30, 25, 20, 15, 10, 5, 0.

Key Stage 1 Number Fun

Perfect Pizza Parlour

Numeracy Objective Link - Fractions

Year 2: Begin to recognise and find one half and one quarter of shapes and small numbers of objects.

Begin to recognise that two halves or four quarters make one whole and that two quarters and one half are equivalent.

Year 3: **Find fractions of shapes and numbers.**

Begin to recognise simple equivalent fractions: for example, five tenths and one half, five fifths and one whole.

Presentation and Prop Ideas

➢ Make big laminated cardboard pizzas. Make at least 2 half pizza and 4 quarter pizza slices which can then be used to represent the different verses in the song. Use these props to help the children visualise the fractions as you sing the song.

➢ Make a big space in the middle of the classroom, or use the hall. Ask children to lie down on the floor with their feet in the middle and hands stretched out in groups of 4. For each group you will also need another child who can represent the chef at the 'Perfect Pizza Parlour' The children who are pretending to be the pizza in the song are then chopped up by the chef!

Adaptations and Extensions

➢ Extend the song by writing lyrics which will include other fractions. For example, 'Half a pizza, cut in quarters - 4 equal eighths'!

Actions

The children can pretend to use a pizza cutter during the chorus and then use their fingers to represent the fractions. For example: whole pizza is 4 fingers, half a pizza is 2 fingers and a quarter pizza is 1 finger.

Links

This is the only song from b
Resource Packs which cove
Fractions.

Oliver and Imogen ready for action!
(Photo © Andy Smith)

Key Stage 1 Number Fun

Perfect Pizza Parlour
(Fractions)

Welcome to the Number Fun,
Perfect Pizza Parlour!
We will chop your pizzas up,
So you can taste the flavour!

Verse 1:   1 pizza cut in half,
    - 2 equal pieces.
    1 pizza cut in half,
    - 2 equal pieces.

Verse 2:   1 pizza cut in quarters,
    - 4 equal pieces!
    1 pizza cut in quarters,
    - 4 equal pieces!

Verse 3:   Half a pizza cut in half,
    - 2 equal quarters.
    Half a pizza cut in half,
    - 2 equal quarters.

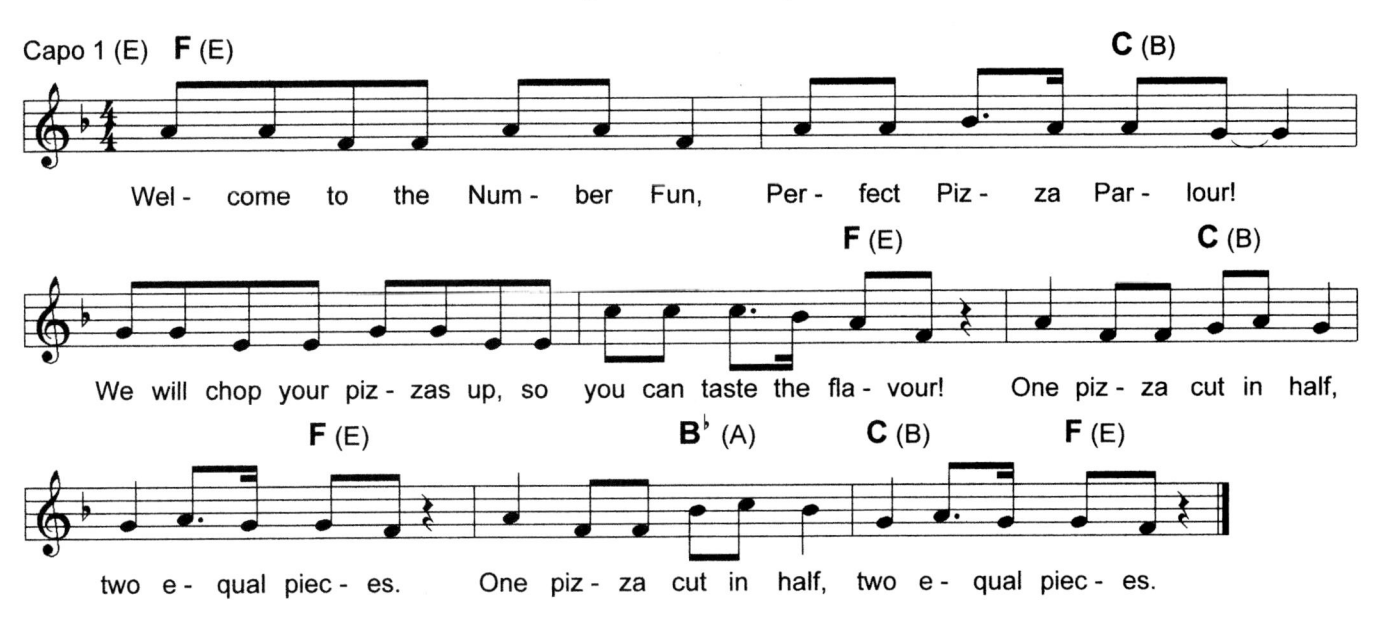

© 2005 Dave Godfrey, Omega Zone Publishing
Please note: This is not a photocopyable resource

Safe in the Barn

Numeracy Objective Link - Counting On from 0 to 10

F Stage: **Say and use the number names in order in familiar contexts** such as number rhymes, songs, stories, counting games and activities (first to five, then ten, then twenty and beyond).

Find 1 more or one less than a number from 1 to 10.

Year 1: Know the number names and recite them in order to at least 20, from and back to zero.

Within the range 0-30, say the number that is 1 or 10 more or less than a given number.

Presentation and Prop Ideas

➢ Make a set of sheep hats and choose 10 children to wear them. Dress up one child (or yourself) as Farmer Pete, or Farmer Petula, and place the 10 lost 'sheep' around the room. You may wish to number the children so each child knows when to 'baa!' Sing the song with Farmer Pete choosing one sheep at the end of each verse and welcoming them into the 'barn'.

➢ Purchase or make a set of sheep puppets which the children can then hold to represent the sheep as you present the song in a similar way to the first idea.

➢ Use the 'Farmer Pete's Chicken Song' story-board from the 'Big Teacher Game-board Poster Pack Set 2' and the sheep counters from 'Farmer Pete' story-board found in the 'Big Teacher Game-board Poster Pack Set 1'. Details of both packs can be found on page 53. The story-board has a big barn on it and the small laminated sheep can be initially placed around the farm. As you sing the song, move the sheep one by one into the barn as a visual representation of the song.

➢ Purchase and use the 'Farmer Pete's Chicken Song' file from the 'Number Fun Whiteboard Files' to help present this song. *(Details of this resource can be found on page 53.)*

Adaptations and Extensions

➢ You could change the type of animal in the song. Cattle have worked particularly well.

➢ Instead of only one sheep being found each time, vary the number of sheep which Farmer Pete finds during each verse.

➢ Instead of starting the song at zero, choose another number to start counting from.

Actions

The children will really enjoy acting the song out as suggested above. They can do the most amazing sheep impressions! Why not ask your head-teacher to come and play the part of Farmer Pete?!

Links

Counting On to 10 is also tackled in;
  Song 3: Coins on the Floor
  Song 10: Little Soldiers

From 'Song Resource Pack 1';
  Song 8: Dancing in the Sun
  Song 11: I Can Count (& Spider)

Key Stage 1 Number Fun

Safe in the Barn
(Counting On from 1 to 10)

No little sheep, safe in the barn,
Out of the cold, safe from harm,
Hear a bleat from across the farm,
(Baa! In you come sheepy!)
That's... 1 little sheep safe in the barn!

1 little sheep, safe in the barn,
Out of the cold, safe from harm,
Hear a bleat from across the farm,
(Baa! In you come sheepy!)
That's... 2 little sheep safe in the barn!   Etc...

9 little sheep, safe in the barn,
Out of the cold, safe from harm,
Hear a bleat from across the farm,
(Baa! In you come sheepy!)
That's... 10 little sheep safe in the barn!

Safe in the Barn! *(Photo © Andy Smith)*

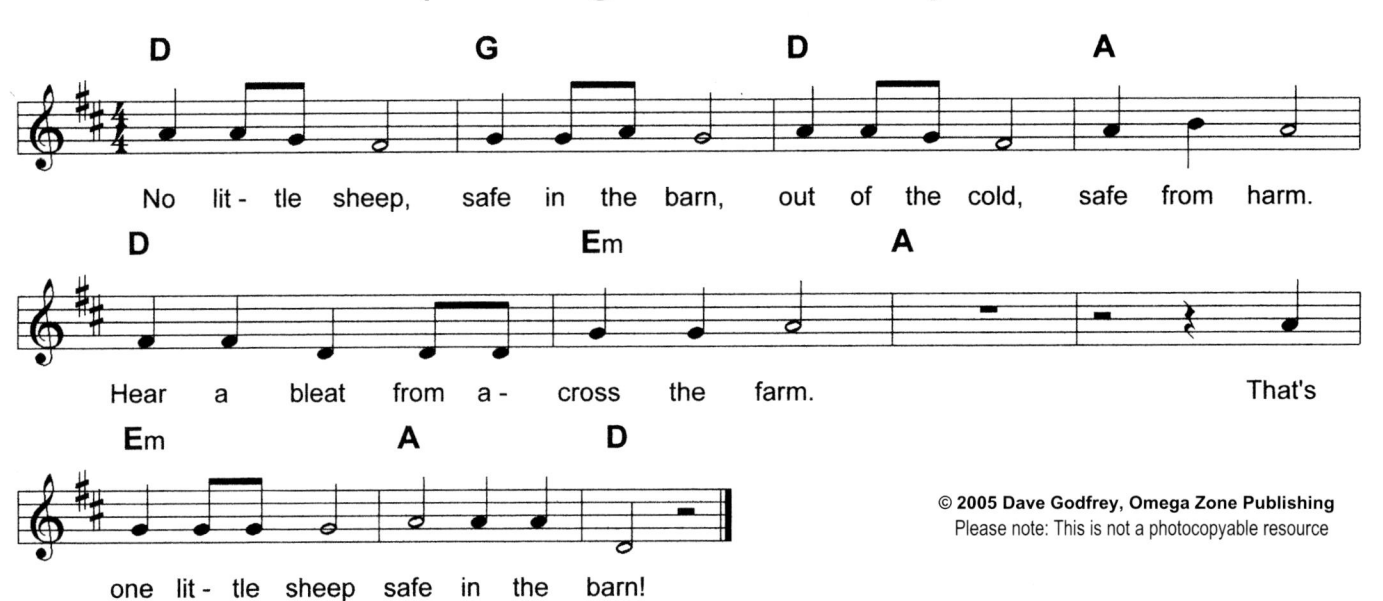

© 2005 Dave Godfrey, Omega Zone Publishing
Please note: This is not a photocopyable resource

Key Stage 1 ★ Number Fun

The Adventures of Rover

Numeracy Objective Link - 2, 5 and 10 Times Tables

Year 2:　　**Know by heart: multiplication facts for the 2 and 10 times-tables.**
　　　　　　Begin to know: multiplication facts for the 5 times-table.
Year 3:　　**Know by heart: multiplication facts for the 2, 5 and 10 times-tables.**

Presentation and Prop Ideas

➢ This is designed to be a fun way of learning the 2, 5 and 10 times tables. The best way to remember it is to add some actions to it. Make up a set of actions which represent the words outlined opposite, similar to the suggested actions below. Working in a clear space, have the children in pairs with one child pretending to be Rover!

➢ Make a set of flashcards or posters with each times table clearly written out. Next to the appropriate calculations add some visual clues to the storyline which runs through the song. Sing the song using the posters to remind the children of the tables.

Adaptations and Extensions

➢ Try making up a different story to accompany the 2, 5 and 10 times tables. Try out some of the best ones as a class.

➢ Try writing some storylines to accompany other times tables. These amended lyrics can then be sung using the backing track.

Actions

Here are a simple set of actions for the 2 times table verse:

Come on Rover, it's walkies!

　　(Pick up the lead and gently pull Rover up from the floor!)

2 x 1 is 2, 2 x 2 is 4, 2 x 3 is 6, Now show me some tricks!

　　(Let Rover off the lead and encourage the dog by clapping a couple of times.)

2 x 4 is 8, 2 x 5 is 10, Rover, I'll tell you when! Good boy!

　　(Pretend to throw Rover a ball, but not release it. Then repeat, releasing the pretend ball.)

2 x 6 is 12, 2 x 7 is 14, 2 x 8 is 16, Oh, go on the Green!

　　(Point to the Green and encourage Rover to go on it!)

2 x 9 is 18, 2 x 10 is 20, Rover, it's time for your tea!

　　(Pretend to put Rover's lead back on to take him back to your home.)

Links

This is the only song in both Song Resource Packs which tackles Times Tables.

Key Stage 1 Number Fun

The Adventures of Rover
(2, 5 and 10 Times-Tables)

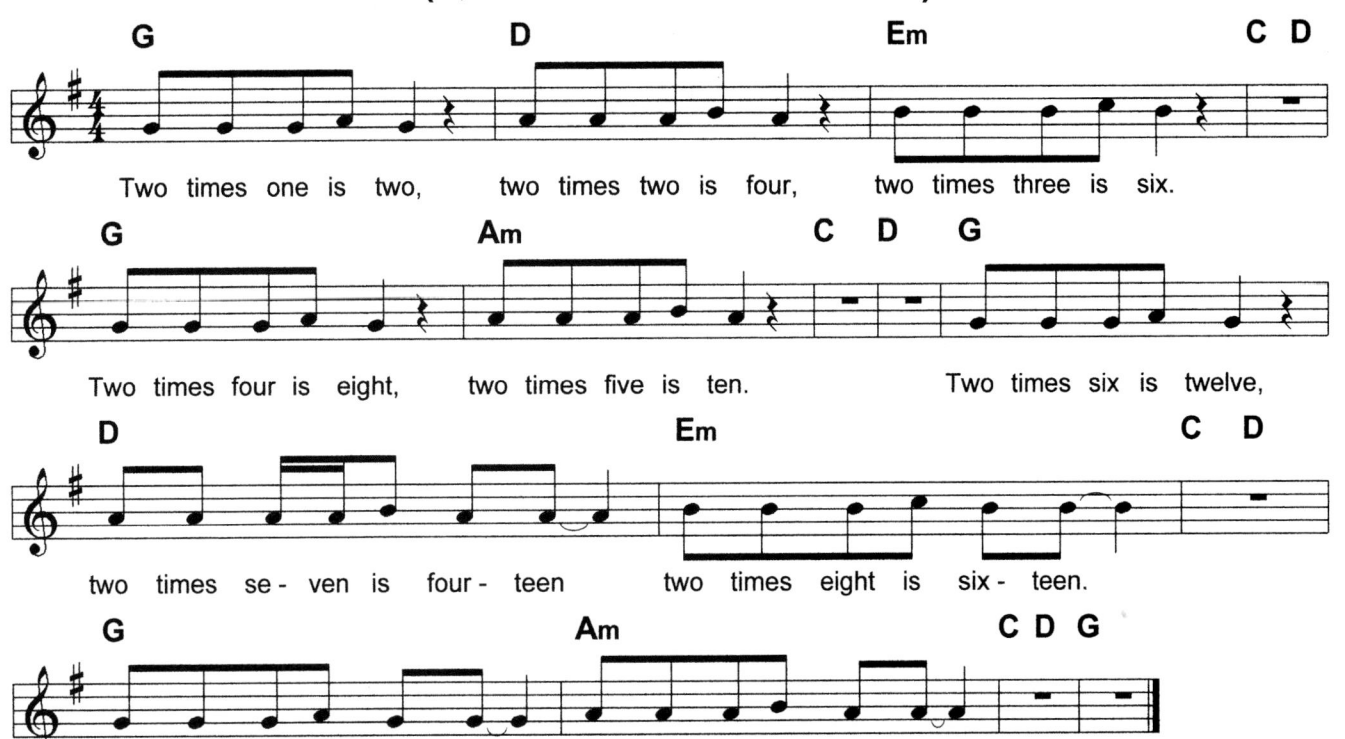

Two times one is two, two times two is four, two times three is six.
Two times four is eight, two times five is ten. Two times six is twelve,
two times seven is fourteen, two times eight is sixteen.
Two times nine is eighteen, two times ten is twenty.

© 2005 Dave Godfrey, Omega Zone Publishing
Please note: This is not a photocopyable resource

2 x Table: Walkies!
2 x 1 is 2, 2 x 2 is 4, 2 x 3 is 6, Now show me some tricks!
2 x 4 is 8, 2 x 5 is 10, Rover, I'll tell you when! Good boy!
2 x 6 is 12, 2 x 7 is 14, 2 x 8 is 16, Oh, go on the Green!
2 x 9 is 18, 2 x 10 is 20, Rover, it's time for your tea!

5 x Table: Tea-time!
5 x 1 is 5, 5 x 2 is 10, 5 x 3 is 15, Now lick it up clean!
5 x 4 is 20, 5 x 5 is 25, Rover - leave fishy alive! Bad boy!
5 x 6 is 30, 5 x 7 is 35, 5 x 8 is 40, Give fishy to me!
5 x 9 is 45, 5 x 10 is 50, Rover, it's time for TV!

10 x Table: TV-time!
10 x 1 is 10, 10 x 2 is 20, 10 x 3 is 30, It's CBBC!
10 x 4 is 40, 10 x 5 is 50, Rover, sit on my knee. Good boy!
10 x 6 is 60, 10 x 7 is 70, 10 x 8 is 80, Do you need a wee?
10 x 9 is 90, 10 x 10 is 100, Rover, it's walkies then bed!

Key Stage 1 ★ Number Fun

The Difference

Numeracy Objective Link - Difference

Year 1: **Understand the operation of subtraction as 'difference'.**
Year 2: Find a small difference by counting up from the smaller to the larger number.
Year 3: Find a small difference by counting up from the smaller to the larger number.

Presentation and Prop Ideas

➢ Purchase, or borrow, a beret. You (or a child) can then pretend to be the French teacher who has got so many poorly children! Ask some of the children to stand one side of you to represent the children who are well - they should have a beaming smile on their faces. Ask another group of children to stand on the other side of you to represent the children who are poorly - these should look very sick and should be holding their tummies! Sing the song as a class, with the children acting as a visual reference for those still sitting down.

➢ Make a story-board to help present the story. The children and the teacher could be illustrated using pieces of clipart which are printed out and laminated. Again this will make an excellent visual aid for telling the story of the song.

➢ Prepare a set of flashcards with lines of happy and sad faces on. These can then become a visual representation of the difference you are calculating. The children will find it most helpful if the happy and sad faces are in lines above and below each other.

Adaptations and Extensions

➢ For those children who need stretching, use the backing track version of the song and sing it using harder numbers.

Actions

As suggested above, the children could pretend to play the characters involved in the story. The French teacher could wear some appropriate national dress. The well children can have a big smile on their faces and the poorly children should pretend to be suitably ill!

Links

This is the only song which is specifically designed to practise difference. Other songs which practise subtraction include Song 4: Farmer Pete's Chicken Song.

Key Stage 1 Number Fun

The Difference
(Difference)

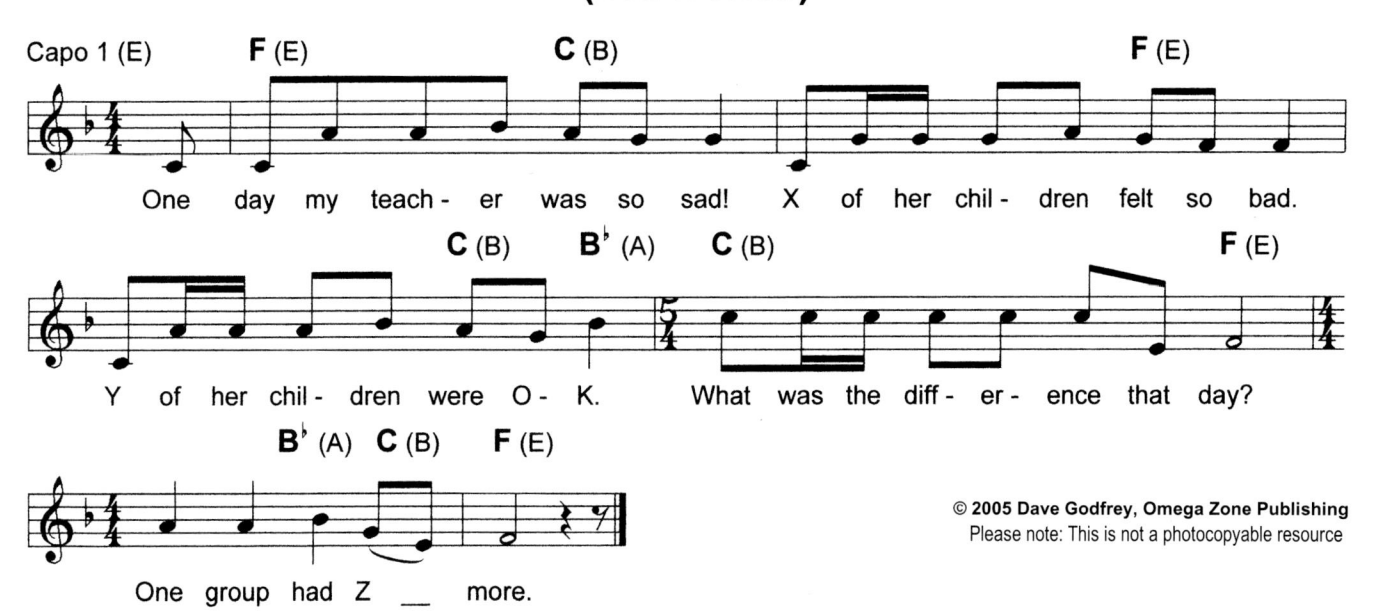

One day my teacher was so sad!
X of her children felt so bad.
Y of her children were OK.
What was the difference that day?
One group had (X - Y or Y - X) more.

© 2005 Dave Godfrey, Omega Zone Publishing
Please note: This is not a photocopyable resource

Key Stage 1 Number Fun

The Keep Fit Song

Numeracy Objective Link - Position Vocabulary

F Stage: **Use everyday words to describe position**, direction and movement: for example, follow and give instructions about positions, directions and movements in PE and other activities.

Year 1: Use everyday language to describe position, direction and movement. Make whole turns and half turns.

Year 2: **Use mathematical vocabulary to describe position, direction and movement**. Recognise whole, half and quarter turns, to the left or right, clockwise or anti-clockwise.

Presentation and Prop Ideas

➢ It is designed to help the children practise their positional vocabulary. It would be very difficult to do this song sitting down so find a big space either in the classroom or in the hall. The children will need to work with a partner. Walk through the song as outlined below and then use the CD track. This song uniquely combines P.E., Maths and Music for cross-curricular bonus points!

Adaptations and Extensions

➢ Re-write the lyrics of the song using other position vocabulary and present it using the backing track version of the song.

Actions

Intro: *Put a smile on your face, put the twinkle in your toes, put the frizz back in your hair!*
(Smile, dance on your toes and then frizz up your hair!)

Come and sing along, with the Keep Fit Song and bounce high in the air!
(Dance and then bounce!)

Chorus: *This is the Number Fun, Keep Fit song, do your exercising as you sing along!*
(Make up with a simple routine to use during each chorus!)

Verses: *Walk forwards, walk backwards (x3), and do it to the funky beat!*
(Simply move forward 4 steps and back 4 three times, then criss-cross legs!)

To the left now, to the right now, (x3), and do it to the funky beat!
(Move 4 steps to the right then 4 to the left, three times, then criss-cross legs!)

Crawl under, walk over, (x3), and do it to the funky beat!
(Working with a partner, one crawls between partners legs, then criss-cross!)

Move closer, apart now, (x3), and do it to the funky beat!
(Working with a partner move together and apart, then criss-cross legs!)

Roll, turn, stretch, bend, (x3), and do it to the funky beat!
(Roll hands over, turn 90°, stretch high, bend at knees, then criss-cross legs!)

Links

This is the only song in both Song Resource Packs which tackles Position Vocabulary.

Key Stage 1 Number Fun

The Keep Fit Song
(Position Vocabulary)

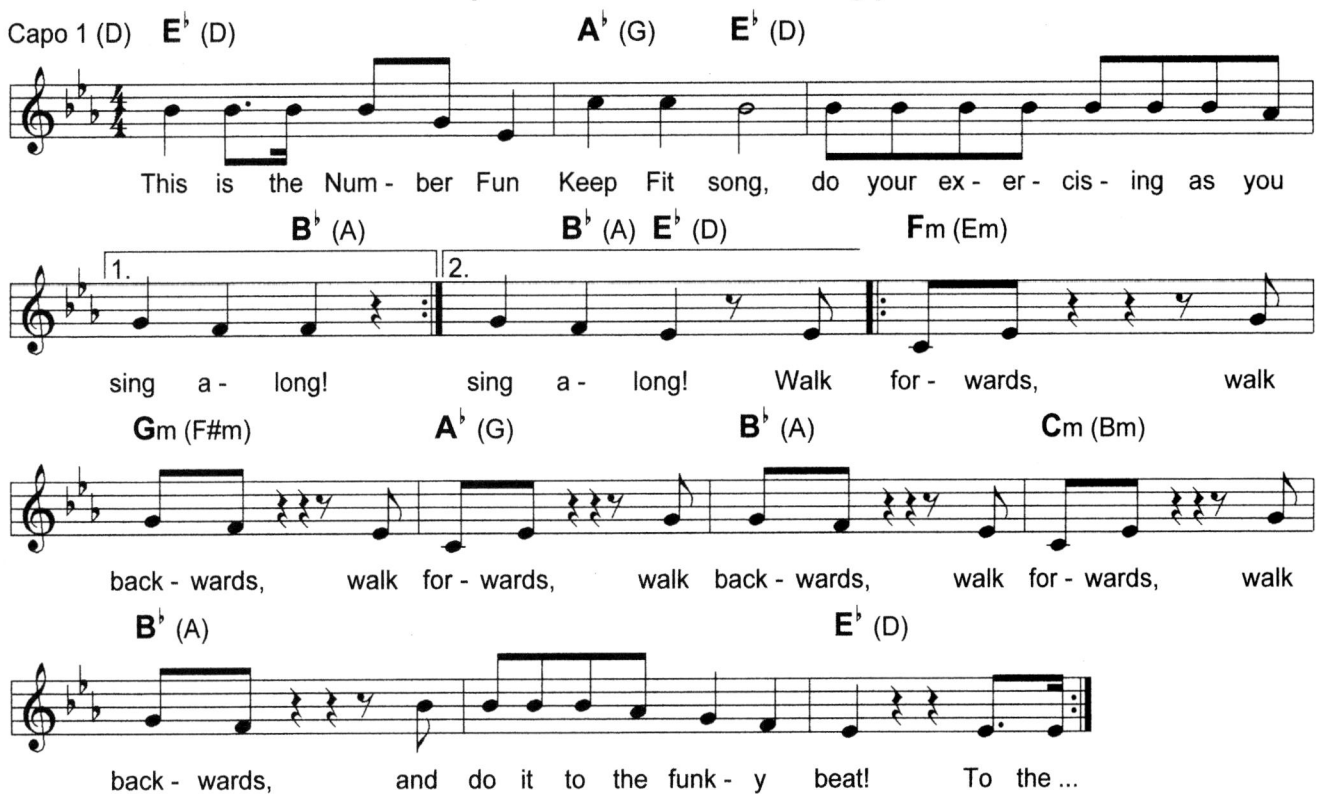

*Put a smile on your face, put the twinkle in your toes,
Put the frizz back in your hair, oh yeah!
Come and sing along with the Keep Fit Song,
And bounce high in the air!*

**This is the Number Fun Keep Fit song,
Do your exercising as you sing along! (x2)**

Walk forwards, walk backwards (x3) and do it to the funky beat!

To the left now, to the right now, (x3) and do it to the funky beat!

Crawl under, walk over, (x3) and do it to the funky beat!

Move closer, apart now, (x3) and do it to the funky beat!

Roll, turn, stretch, bend, (x3) and do it to the funky beat!

© 2005 Dave Godfrey, Omega Zone Publishing
Please note: This is not a photocopyable resource

Key Stage 1 Number Fun

Tick Tock

Numeracy Objective Link - Recognising Clock Times

F Stage: Begin to read o'clock time.
Year 1: Read the time to the hour or half hour on analogue clocks.
Year 2: Read the time to the hour, half hour or quarter hour on an analogue clock.

Presentation and Prop Ideas

➢ The simplest way of presenting this song is to use a teacher clock. You are then in control of the times you set and the children can see clearly where the hour hand and the minute hand are pointing. The children then sing according to the clock face they can see.

➢ A more kinaesthetic presentation would be to make a 'human clock'. Give 12 children some flashcards with the numbers 1 - 12 on. The children are then asked to sit in a circle. Choose two children to represent the hour and minute hands, providing each children with a large cardboard 'hour hand' or 'minute hand' to lay along their body. You, or a child if they are leading the song, can then position the 'hands' by lying them on the floor. Encourage the rest of the class to stand around the 'human clock' and to join in the song!

➢ Give the children their own clock and ask them to show you the time as you sing each verse.

Adaptations and Extensions

➢ For Y3's or able younger children you might wish to extend and adapt the song to allow for intervals of 5 minutes. E.g. 'When the big hand points to 1, and the small hands just past 4...'

Actions

As well as acting out the song as suggested above, you could ask the children to move the lower part of their arms like a pendulum in time with the rhythm of the song. It is worth noting that the song is recorded at 60 beats per minute, which means each beat is exactly one second!

Links

Other songs which tackle Time concepts are;
Song 7: In a Week
Song 9: January, February

From 'Song Resource Pack 1';
Song 1: 31 Days in January
Song 7: Counting Time
Song 21: The Story of My Day

(Photo © Andy Smith)

Key Stage 1 ★ Number Fun

Tick Tock
(Recognising Clock Times)

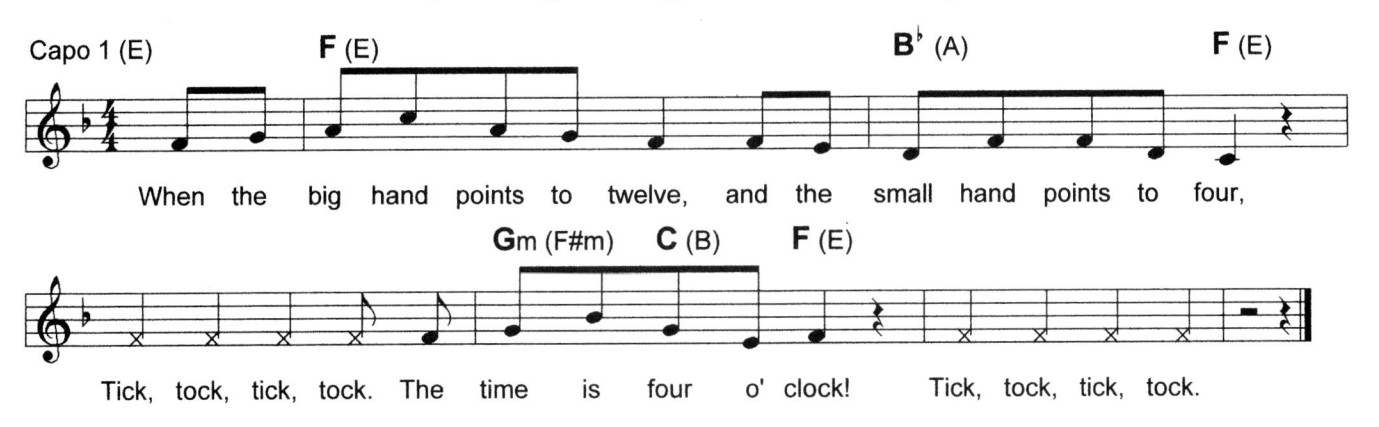

Capo 1 (E)

When the big hand points to twelve, and the small hand points to four,
Tick, tock, tick, tock. The time is four o' clock! Tick, tock, tick, tock.

© 2005 Dave Godfrey, Omega Zone Publishing
Please note: This is not a photocopyable resource

When the big hand points to 12,
And the small hand points to 4,
Tick, tock, tick, tock,
The time is 4 o'clock!
Tick, tock, tick, tock.

Adaptations:

When the big hand points to 6,
And the small one's just past 2,
... The time is half past 2!

When the big hand points to 9,
And the small one's near to 5,
... The time is quarter to 5!

When the big hand points to 3,
And the small one's just past 1,
... The time is quarter past 1!

Key Stage 1 — Number Fun

The Celebration Song

Song Objectives - Recognition and Celebration

All Ages: To recognise and celebrate both class work and individual work.
            To build up the levels of class esteem, and self esteem of individual pupils.

Presentation and Prop Ideas

➢ Use existing resources or design a celebration sticker, badge, certificate or hat to present to the individual children who have worked really hard on their Number Fun work. There are two photocopyable Number Fun certificates in the back of the first Activity Resource Pack which are designed for this purpose. The certificates, or other rewards, can be presented to the children as you sing the song.

➢ Add some actions - see the Actions section below.

Adaptations and Extensions

➢ You could change the third line of the song to include the specific skill that you have been practising that day. For example, 'You have practised skills' could become, 'You have counted on' etc.

➢ You could use this song in other areas of the curriculum to celebrate the achievements of the class.

Actions

We will celebrate our (child's name/Number Fun) work! Well done, well done. (x2)
   (Shaking hands with specific child or other children in class. You could add some clapping.)

You have practised skills,
   (Clap three times on <u>pract</u> - <u>ised</u> - <u>skills</u>)

Thought things through,
   (Point both index finger to the temple of the brain)

Worked really hard,
   (Pretend to write really hard on piece of paper, with head down)

So good for you!
   (Double 'thumbs-up')

We'll celebrate our (child's name/Number Fun) work! Well done, well done.
   (Shaking hands and clapping.)

Links

Celebration of work is a powerful way of motivating and rewarding the children. The use of celebrating to music is specifically encouraged in the 'Accelerated Learning for Primary Schools' by Alistair Smith and Nicola Call (see Introduction).

> We used this song to celebrate our Literacy and Numeracy work. I would like to use it in our celebration school assembly.
> B Charles, Y3 teacher

Key Stage 1 • Number Fun

The Celebration Song
(Recognising and Celebrating Achievement)

[Sheet music with chords: Capo 1 (E), F (E), C (B), B♭ (A), C (B), etc.]

Lyrics under music:
We will cel-e-brate our X X's work! Well done __, well done. We will cel-e-brate our X X's work! Well done __, well done. You have prac-tised skills, thought things through, worked real-ly hard, so good for you! We'll cel-e-brate our X X's work! Well done __, well done.

We will celebrate our *(name of child)*'s work!
Well done, well done. (x2)
You have practised skills, thought things through,
Worked really hard, so good for you!
We'll celebrate our *(name of child)*'s work!
Well done, well done.

We will celebrate our Number Fun!
Well done, well done. (x2)
We have practised skills, thought things through,
Worked really hard, so good for you!
We'll celebrate our Number Fun!
Well done, well done.

© 2005 Dave Godfrey, Omega Zone Publishing
Please note: This is not a photocopyable resource

* Note: The recorded track uses the names of the author's children; Timothy, Anna and Esther.

Key Stage 1 • Number Fun

Number Fun Resource Packs

Song Resource Pack 1
Equipping you to present and teach all 22 songs!

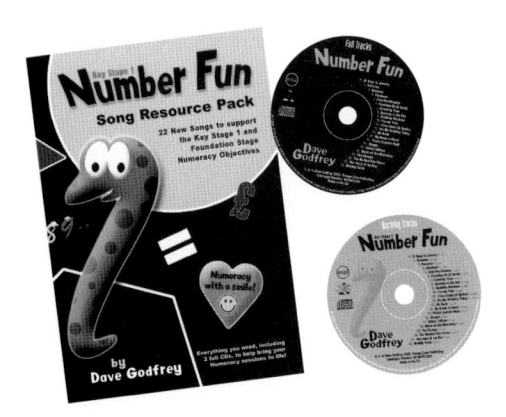

By Dave Godfrey, 2003

54 Page Resource Book full of great presentation ideas, including:

- ✓ Music Score and Song Words
- ✓ Numeracy Objectives
- ✓ Presentation and Prop Ideas
- ✓ Adaptations and Extension Ideas
- ✓ Simple Actions
- ✓ Links between all 22 songs

Pack includes both Full Track and Backing Track CDs featuring all 22 songs.

Themes include; Counting, Place Value, Ordering, Money, Time, Addition and Subtraction, Doubling and Halving, Shape, Number Bonds, Measuring Units ...

Activity Resource Pack 1
Equipping you to lead creative lessons with all 22 songs!

By Dave Godfrey & Rachel Carr 2004

54 Page Resource Book full of creative lesson ideas and photocopyable resources for each song from 'Song Resource Pack 1', including:

- ✓ Warm ups
- ✓ Games
- ✓ Activities
- ✓ Plenary Ideas
- ✓ Photocopyable Resources
- ✓ Tool Kit

Pack includes 12, double sided, full colour, laminated game-boards and 112 double sided, gloss laminated, sheep and sticky toffee counters!

('Complete Resource Set 1' contains both the resources described above.)

Arriving in January 2006:
'Activity Resource Pack 2'
More creative lessons ideas and games to support the teaching of the songs in the **'Song Resource Pack 2'**

For an up-to-date list of resources visit:
www.numberfun.co.uk

Key Stage 1 Number Fun

Supporting Resources

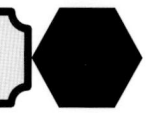

Interactive Whiteboard Files
Bringing the Number Fun songs to life on your computer and on your whiteboard!

This computer software pack features all the great Number Fun graphics, and includes:

- ✓ 'Interactive Whiteboard Files' for 10 Number Fun Songs
- ✓ Words for all 45 songs in both 'Microsoft Word' and 'Smart Notepad' formats

Each **'Interactive Whiteboard File'** has three levels:

1. **CD Presentation** (Pre-programmed to help present the recorded track.)
2. **Semi-Automatic** (You decide what verses or values you wish to present.)
3. **Fully Interactive** (You have complete control over the characters and functions.)

Interactive Whiteboard Files (for songs from Song Resource Pack 1):
- Doubling Machine, Farmer Pete, Russ and His Bus, Sticky Toffees

Interactive Whiteboard Files (for songs from Song Resource Pack 2):
- Cheeky Monkey's Counting Song, Clap Snap, Number Bond (006/004), Number Fun Rocket, Safe in the Barn and Farmer Pete's Chicken Song

Teacher Game-board Poster Packs
Large A1 sized posters, each containing 1 BIG (700mm x 494 mm) Game-board and 18 BIG (70mm) counters!

These are BIG full-colour versions of the game-boards featured in the Activity Resource Packs for you and your children to use.

Simply cut-out the BIG counters and laminate them. Also cut-out the BIG poster and either have it professionally laminated or protect it with sticky back plastic.

Poster Pack 1 includes 4 BIG Posters:
- ✓ Doubling Machine
- ✓ Farmer Pete
- ✓ Russ and His Bus
- ✓ Sticky Toffees

Poster Pack 2 includes 4 BIG Posters:
- ✓ Cheeky Monkey's Counting Song
- ✓ Farmer Pete's Chicken Song
- ✓ Number Bond (006/004)
- ✓ Number Fun Rocket

Complete Poster Pack includes all 8 BIG Number Fun posters!

Other Resources:

32" Inflatable Bananas
(For use with Song 3: Bananas - from 'Song Resource Pack 1')

Extra Game-board Pack
(12 double sided, laminated A4 game-boards with 112 counters - from 'Activity Resource Pack 1')

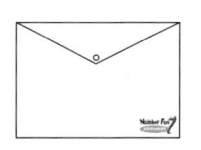

'It's My Birthday' Presentation Pack
(16 x 15mm birthday badges &
1 x 150mm 'It's My Birthday' badge, to help present
Song 12: It's My Birthday, 'Song Resource Pack 1'.)

Resources Folder
(Plastic Folder which holds and protects a Complete Resource Set)

Key Stage 1 - Number Fun

Collective Worship Resources

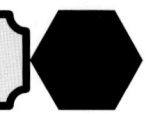

On the Shoulders of Giants
By Dave Godfrey, 2001

12 Numeracy based Christian Collective Worship songs!

This exciting Collective Worship song resource contains:

- ✓ 12 Numeracy linked, Collective Worship songs for Primary Schools
- ✓ Sheet Music with Guitar Chords
- ✓ Acetate Masters
- ✓ Actions
- ✓ CD containing both Full and Backing Track versions of each song

The song resource was written to accompany 'Assemblies that Count' - an assembly resource book which contains 22 Numeracy based primary assembly outlines. (also published by The Stapleford Centre)

Shoulders Teacher Pack includes both 'On the Shoulders of Giants' and 'Assemblies that Count'.

Ordering Number Fun Resources

You can download the up-to-date **Number Fun Order Form** from the **Number Fun website**. This can then be either posted or faxed to the Omega Zone office.

Payment can be made by cheque with order or by payment of invoice sent with goods.

Alternatively, you can also order any of the Number Fun Resources directly, by phoning the **Omega Zone** office on **01904 778848**.

www.numberfun.co.uk

Omega Zone Publishing
PO Box 94,
Copmanthorpe
York, YO23 3WW
Tel/Fax:
01904 778848

Booking a Number Fun Activity Day

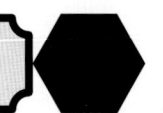

Dave Godfrey travels to Teacher Training events and to schools to present his exciting Number Fun material.

A school 'Key Stage 1 - Number Fun Activity Day' could include:

- ✓ Numeracy based Collective Worship for the whole school
- ✓ Fun-packed sessions for children from Nursery to Y3
- ✓ Whole Staff meeting aimed at equipping teachers to use the Number Fun material

Presentation includes puppetry, role play, magic, props and song actions.

Schools booking a 'Key Stage 1 - Number Fun Activity Day' also receive a free Number Fun Resource Pack of their choice to keep and use in school!

For more details phone 01904 778848 or visit www.numberfun.co.uk.

Key Stage 1 - Number Fun